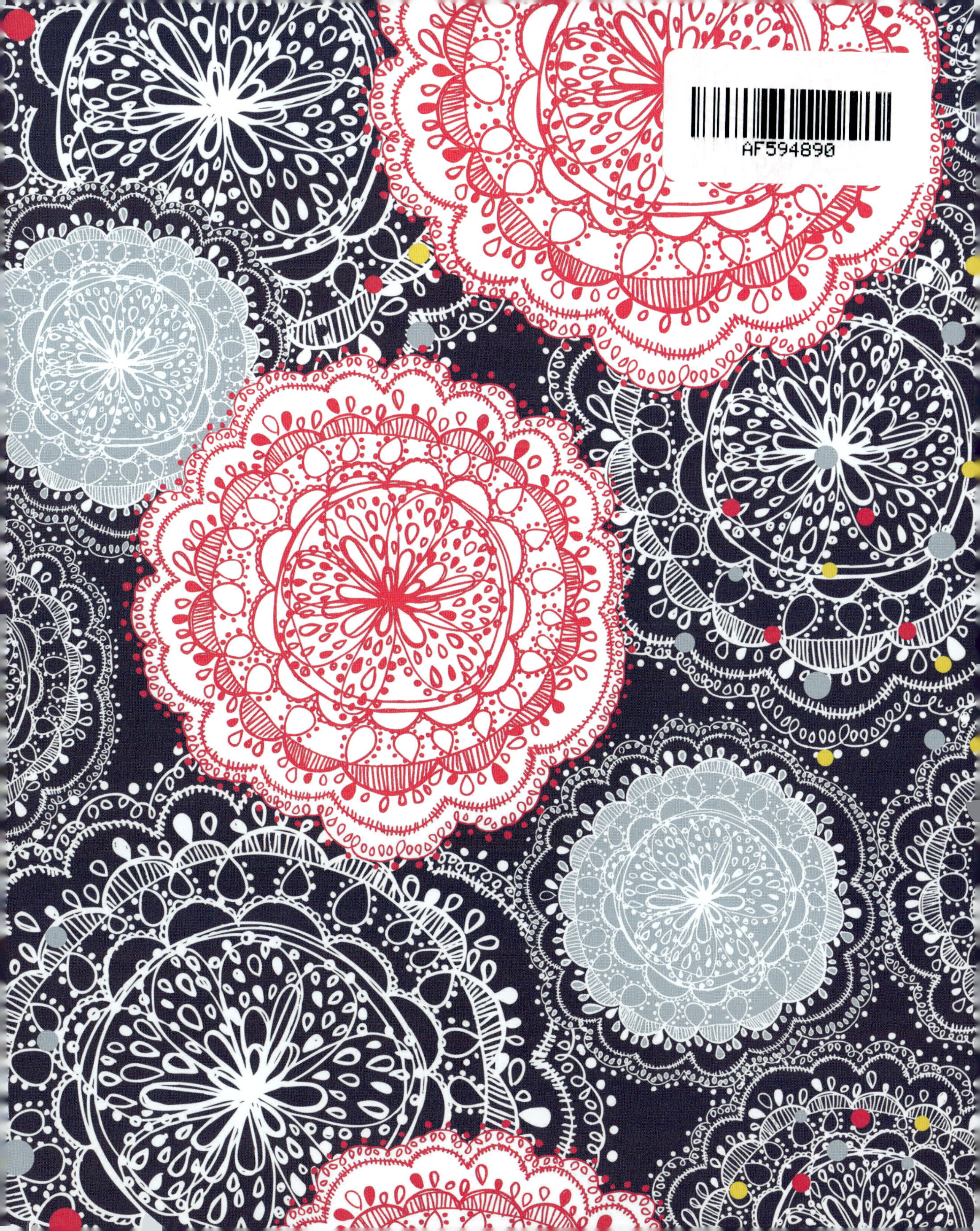

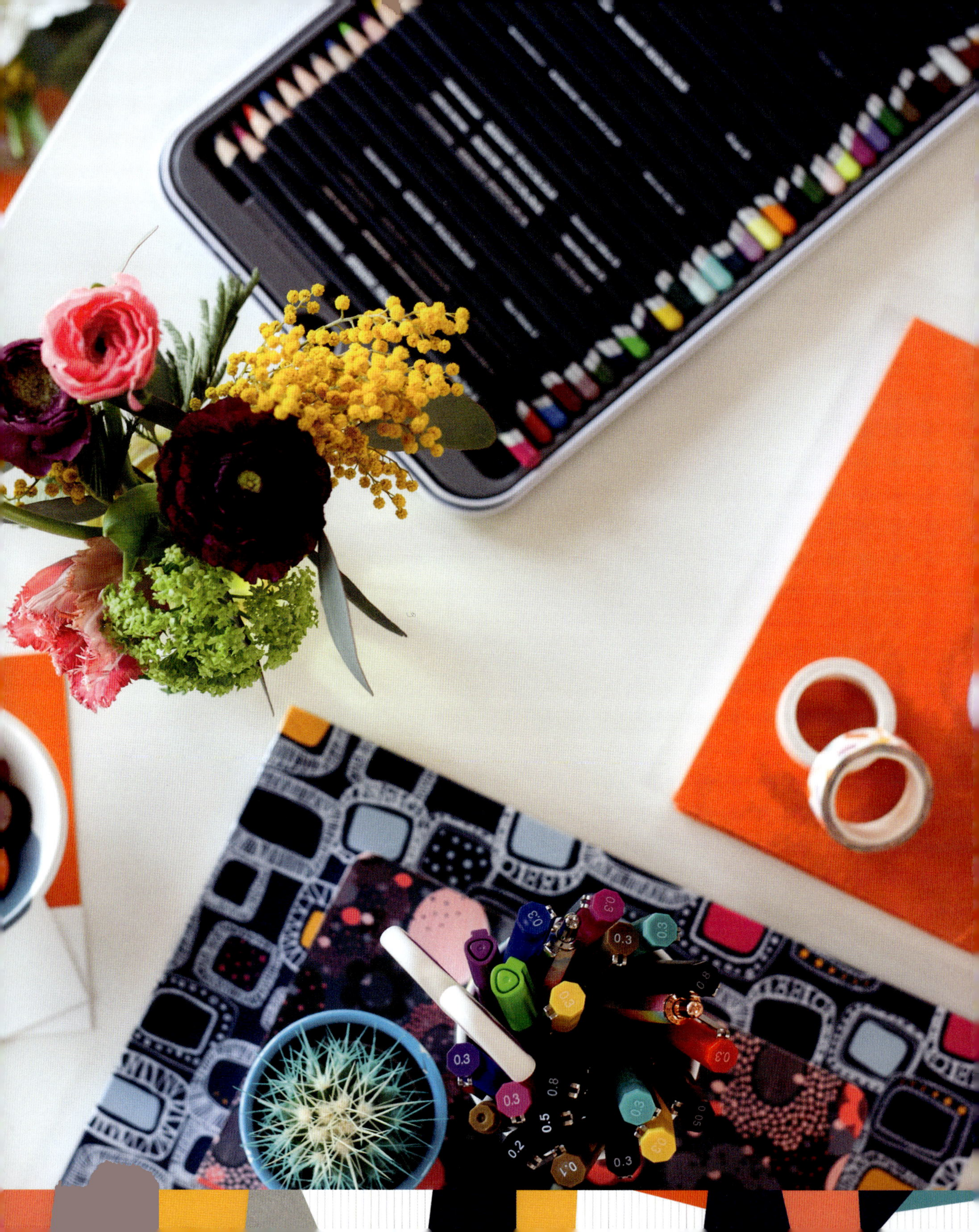

POWER UP YOUR CREATIVITY

Ignite Your Creative Spark

Develop a Productive Practice

Set Goals and Achieve Your Dreams

Rachael Taylor
Cofounder of Make It In Design

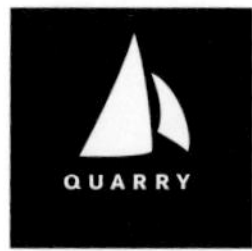

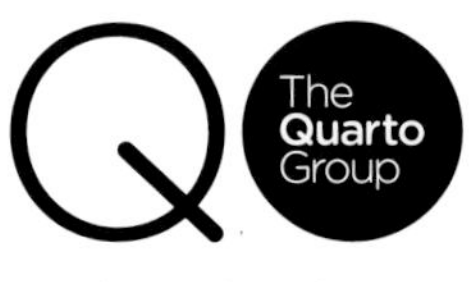

First Published in 2023 by Quarry Books, an imprint of The Quarto Group,
100 Cummings Center, Suite 265-D, Beverly, MA 01915, USA.
T (978) 282-9590 F (978) 283-2742 Quarto.com

10 9 8 7 6 5 4 3 2 1

ISBN: 978-0-7603-7694-2

Digital edition published in 2023
eISBN: 978-0-7603-7695-9

Library of Congress Cataloging-in-Publication Data is available.

Design, cover image and page layout by Rachael Taylor and Kelly Crossley.
Drawings and pattern designs by Rachael Taylor.
All photography by Holly Booth Studio, except for the following: The Struths Photography, pages 30, 33, 101, 120, 122; Fairclough Studios, pages 66, 70, 84, 91, 101, 119; David Diaz pages 101, 111; Shutterstock pages 29, 43, Teresa C Photography page 67, Colin Poole page 101, and Rachael Taylor page 101.

Printed in USA.

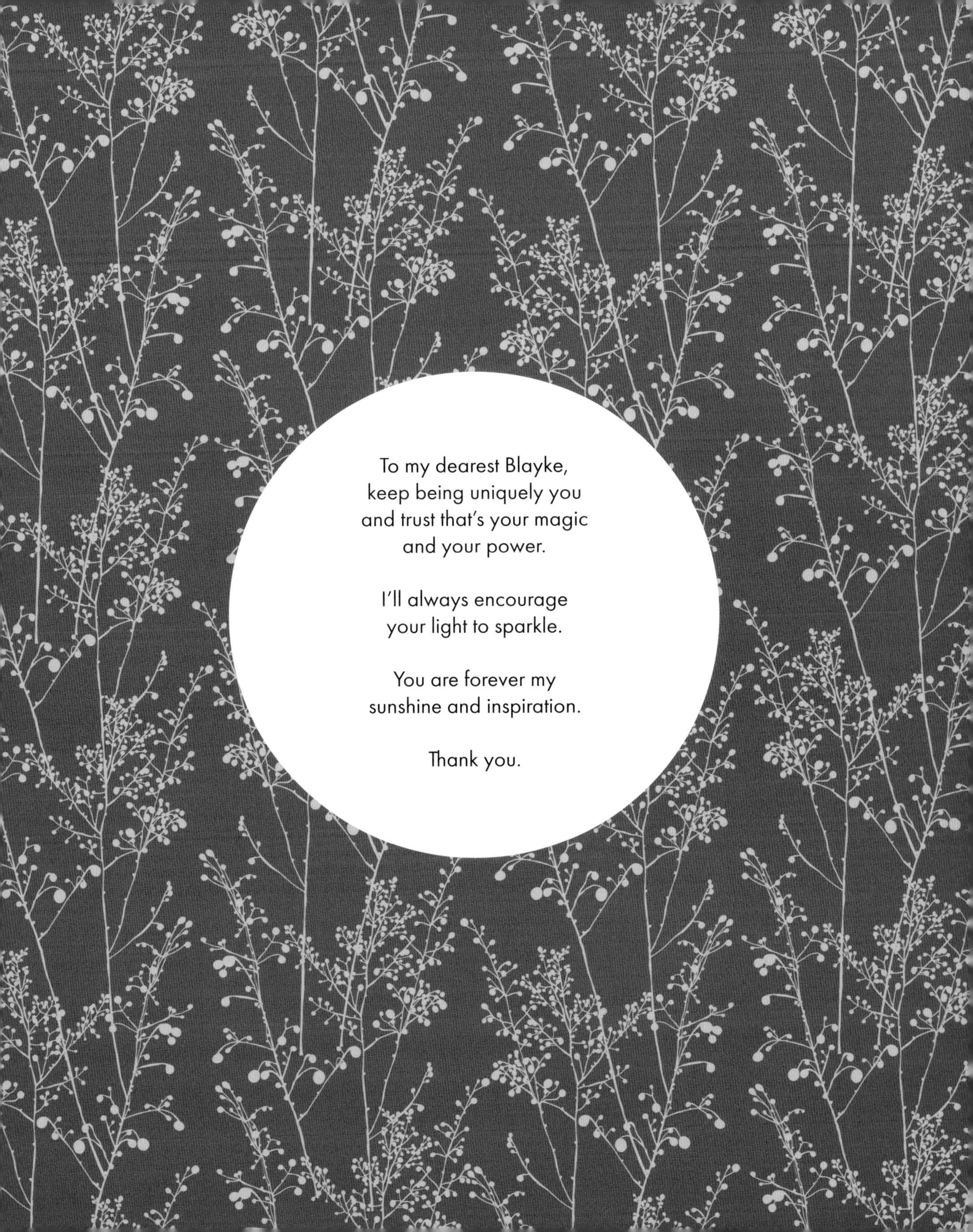

To my dearest Blayke,
keep being uniquely you
and trust that's your magic
and your power.

I'll always encourage
your light to sparkle.

You are forever my
sunshine and inspiration.

Thank you.

CONTENTS

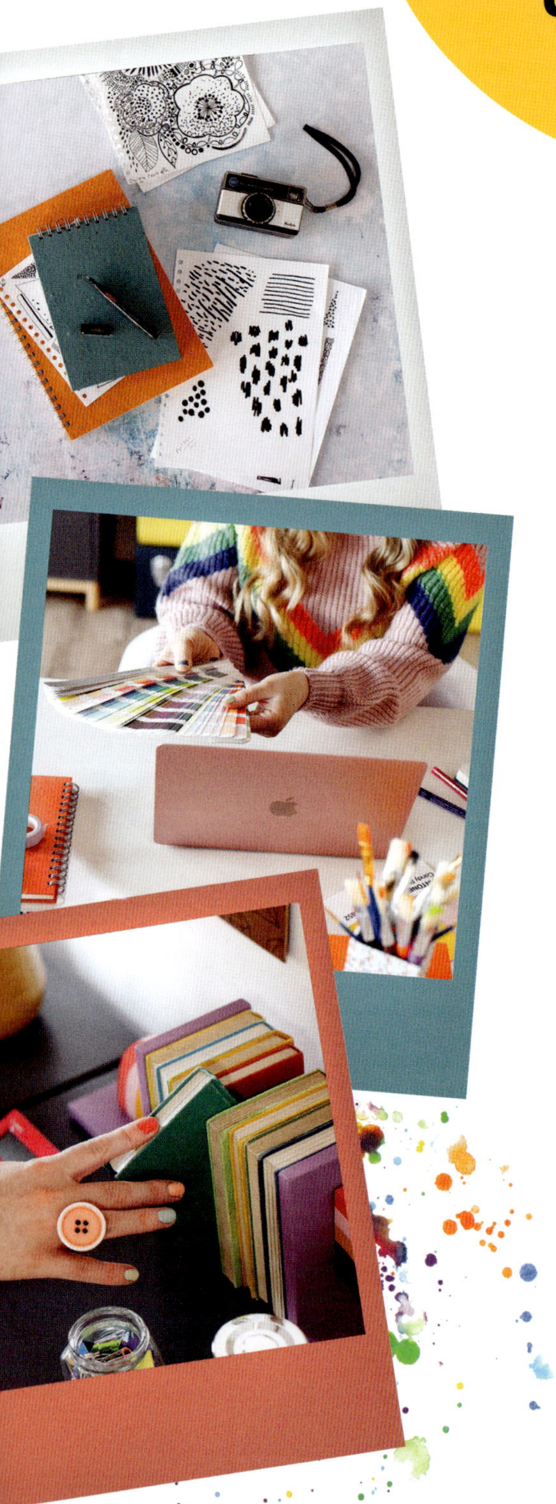

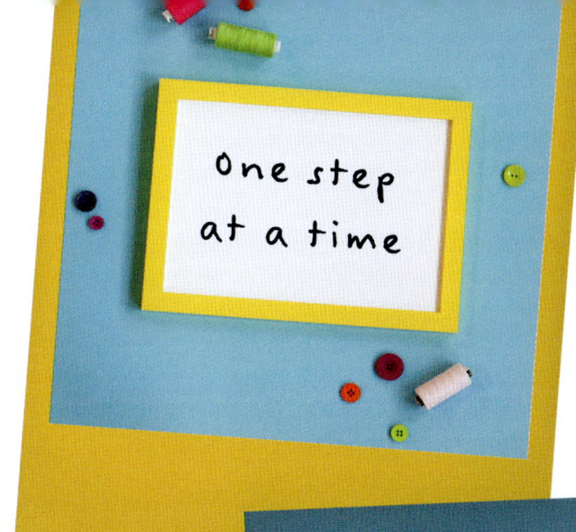
one step
at a time

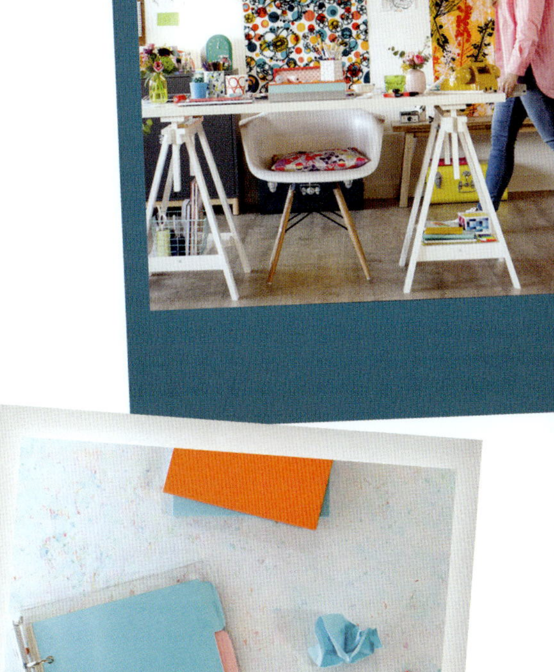

INTRODUCTION

How to use this book

This book is a guide and comfort for your creative soul. It's a mix of prompts, visuals that stimulate, thoughts to ponder, inspiration to gather, and anecdotes to laugh or cry at.

Having lived and breathed creativity from a young age, from performing arts to design, I have experienced quite the roller coaster.

In this book I've reflected upon my career from the past decade and from teaching thousands of creatives worldwide. I believe the powerful conversations I've had with them has aided in unlocking my own creativity. The advice I share can apply to any creative person, aspiring or experienced, no matter where they are on their creative journey, and not just for those who want to pursue a business path.

I've lost my mojo many times, and creativity has been my savior. I recognize how powerful creativity is and how we can use it to help navigate the unpredictable world we live in.

I'm known for speaking from the heart and being chatty. People decribe me as funny, a dreamer yet a realist, an ultimate go-getter, and a ray of positive energy. Yet I've struggled with crippling depression and a troubled life. I'm honest and raw and I don't know another way to be. Professionally these traits run through everything I do, and I once worried about it being a flaw. Yet, with sheer determination, years of honing my talent, keeping a sprinkle of positivity with me, and a lot of hard work, I've achieved the unexpected and built a successful but most importantly ***creative*** life and career. I've learned a lot from this colorful life of mine, and I hope that this insight can help give you the courage to be fearlessly creative.

This book is for ***you*** to support ***you***. I hope you take comfort from it and feel that my words are from those of a friend.

There are ten key themes that work as stand-alone chapters, some longer or shorter than others, but they all feed into one another. I ease you in with how to BEGIN and take you on a journey right through to POWER.

Feel free to approach this book however you want—in one sitting, in bite-size chunks, or when the feeling arises. It might be that you want to highlight moments that resonate, make notes, doodle, scan pages, or even tear pages out and pin them on your wall. You have my full permission to treat the book in any way you want to! Read it on a beach, the sofa, the bus, or even the toilet—it doesn't matter because, hey, I can't see you doing it! What matters most is that you have shown up for yourself just by reading it.

And although this book was made to help you, lovely reader, it's also about giving back. There are many people who have helped me on my journey, and some have been pivotal to helping me keep my creative spark alight (naturally you will find them in the acknowledgments). I recognize that sometimes we just need someone to help bring out the creative gift we have inside of us.

If I can bring you comfort, ignite your creative spark, guide you on your way, be the catalyst for your dream, put a smile on your face on a dark day, or open your mind to new possibilities, then the book has done what it's meant to do. ***I hope it's the beginning of something truly wonderful for you.***

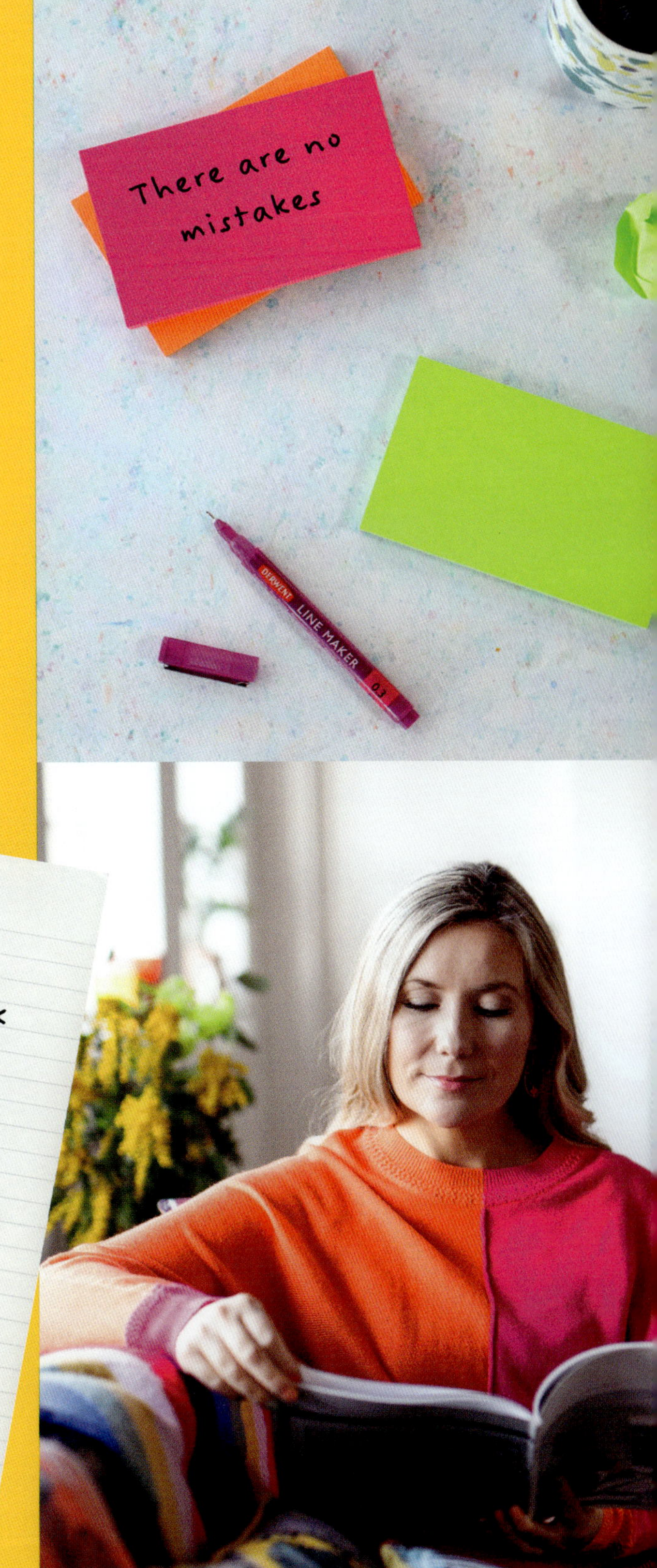

What you'll need:

- A nice hot or cold drink
- An open mind
- A funny bone
- Things to write with
- A cozy seat
- Your intuition
- A smile

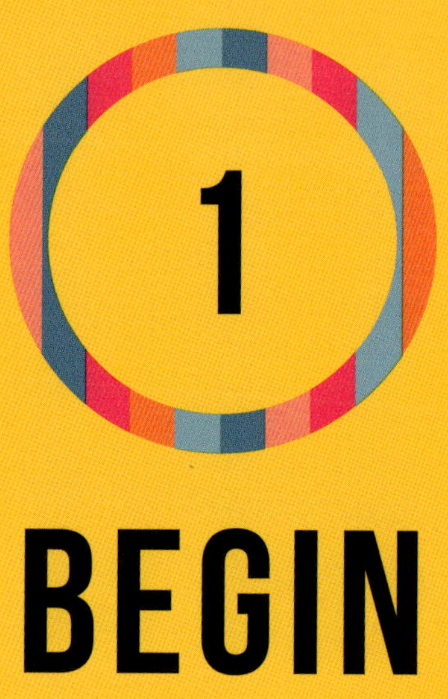

BEGIN

How do I identify where to begin?

The definition of begin
(be-gin) verb;
perform or undergo the first part of (an action or activity).

You are here; you have shown up and made the commitment to begin. Well done you, for recognizing that something isn't sitting quite right and you need a change.

You might be at the beginning of your creative journey or an expert that needs a supercharge, or you might be in a creative rut. In this book we are going to dive in and take a deeper look to find solutions. I promise you we will go very gently to identify what's going on and find ways to help you move forward with your creativity.

This book is an amalgamation of important conversations from my community, conversations in which I kept finding the same obstacles coming up time and again for creative people. Whether you are a hobbyist or design is your main paid profession, we all share many of the same traits and approach experiences in similar ways that can hold us back, even if we don't realize it at the time. For this very reason, this book needed to be written and I too embarked on a brave new and exciting journey as an author. Thank you for taking this path with me.

I want you to have your dreams and goals in mind as we begin to work through the chapters within this book.

Ease yourself in gently but be sure to carve out some time away from the hustle, bustle, and worries of everyday life to begin this all-important process of powering up your creativity.

THOUGHTS TO PONDER ON BEGINNING

Beginning anything can seem daunting. I wanted to take a moment to remind you that everyone was once a beginner. Every completed product, design, or project was once an idea, and those creators were all exactly where you are now. The only difference is that they found a way to turn their dreams into a reality through planning, taking action, and persevering. Some of us will want to take baby steps, others giant leaps; our plans may change or have to be paused unexpectedly, and there is no right or wrong way. No one can take our dreams or vision away from us, and though we all take a different journey, with passion, hard work, and a plan we will eventually get there and achieve our goals. It doesn't matter whether your path was completely different than someone else's. Live for you, not them.

Things can seem so much harder at the beginning, because there's a lot on the to-do list. It can seem overwhelmingly huge and goals can feel out of reach. When I'm starting to get stressed and losing love for the idea I had—even feeling resentment at times—I remind myself that everything always comes together in the end. I tell myself that the process is something I needed to go through and enjoy rather than focusing on just the end goal.

Because life happens during the doing, and it's in the doing that allows us to grow and power up our creativity.

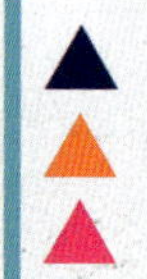

There's beauty in every step of the journey.

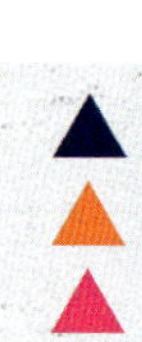

CREATIVE EXERCISES

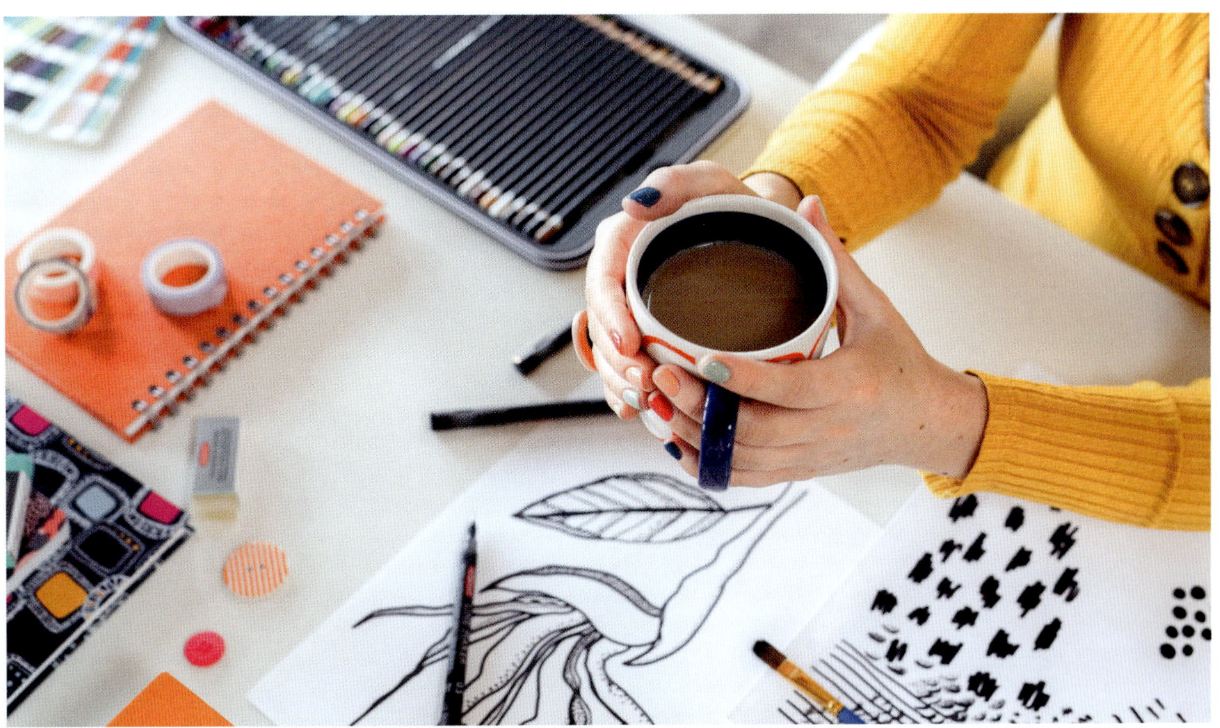

LOOSENING UP

As you begin your journey, I'd love for you to warm up your creative muscles, grab a piece of paper and any pens or pencils that you have nearby, and simply enjoy some art therapy by doodling for five minutes. It can be anything (no one is looking!).

If you get stuck, draw something that regularly inspires you, such as your guitar, your pet, or your favorite flower.

At any point as you are working through this book, I want you to give yourself permission to pause, reflect, and feel free to doodle or whatever form your creativity wants to flow. This is ***your*** journey and creative practice, so do what works for you.

FINISH THE SENTENCE: RIGHT NOW, ON THE SPOT

I love this exercise because it can be a great way to excavate your mind and subconscious. I ask that on the first attempt you just go with your initial thoughts and see what comes out.

I often find that when our true inner voice is free our souls can speak and shine.

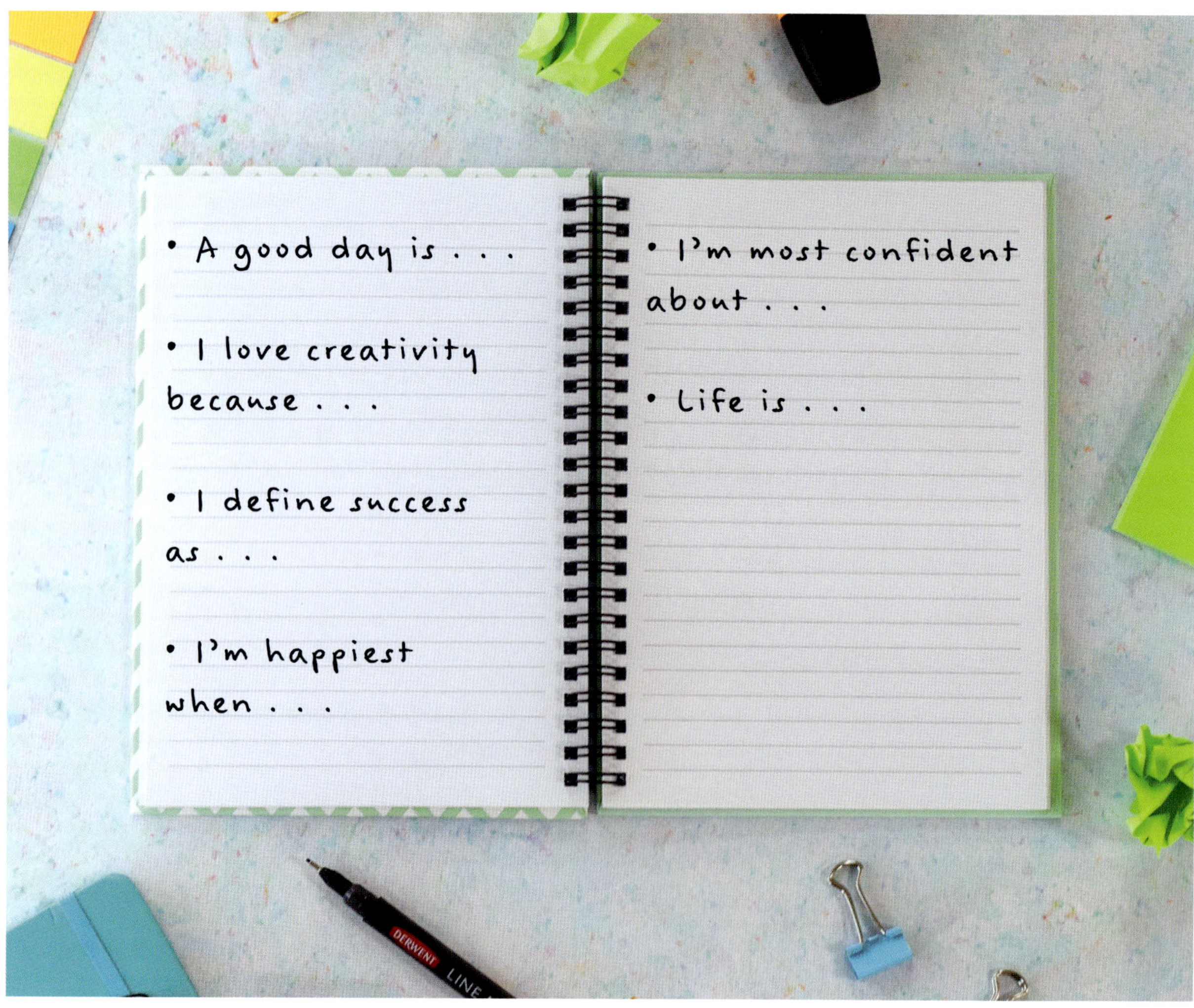

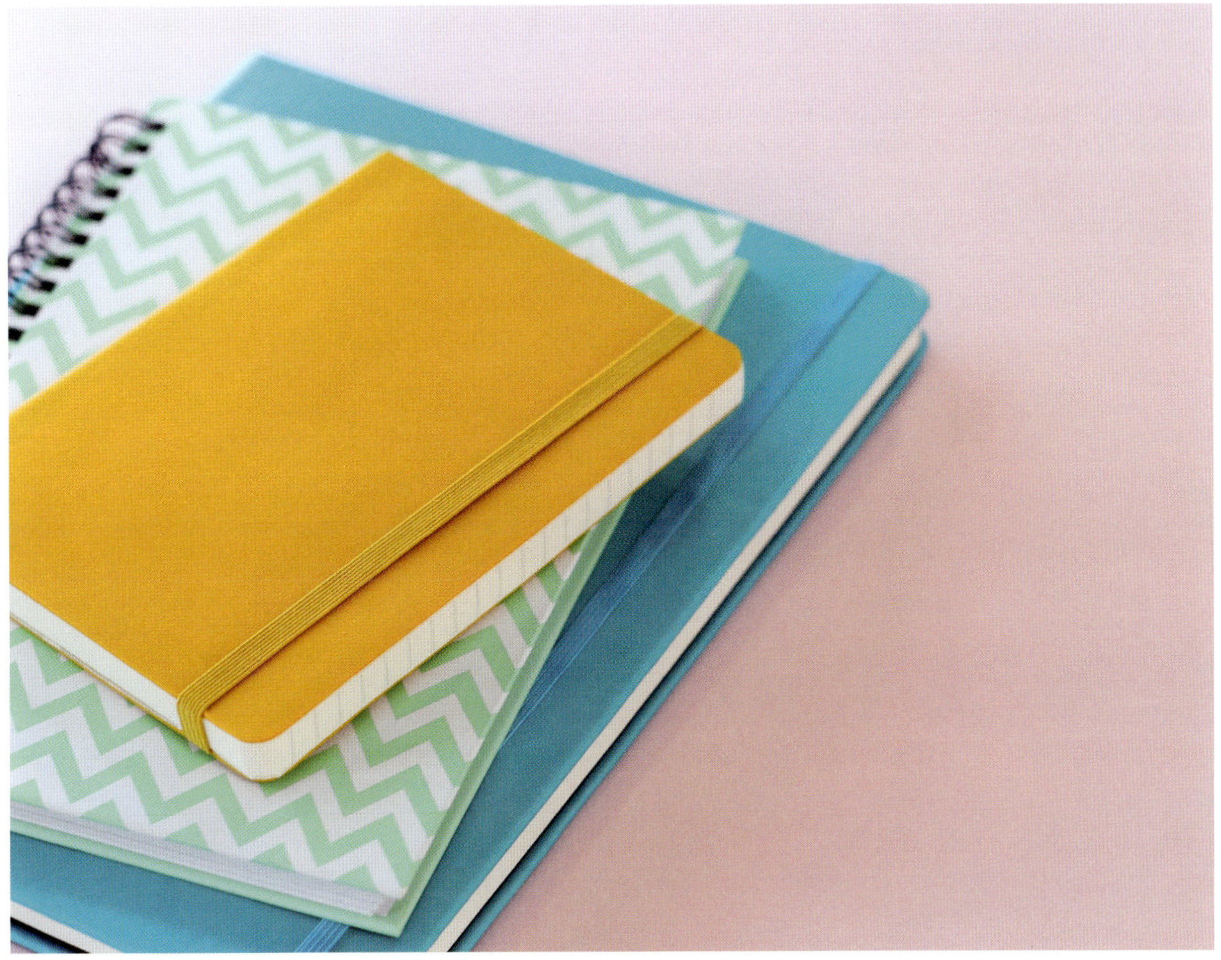

FINISH THE SENTENCE: THINK ABOUT IT

After reviewing your answers, answer the questions again, but this time take a minute to really process your thoughts before putting pen to paper.

- Are there differences? Are there similarities?
- When we begin with something new, or we want to refine something that already exists, it's really important to get clear on our vision.

Enjoy each moment with your actions and activity and try to be fully present.

DREAM CONVERSATION

A very simple task I give many of my clients, students, and friends to start with is to imagine a conversation as if you were a fly on the wall. In that room people are describing your business, art, craft, music—whatever it might be. What do you wish they'd say? What tone would they use? Do they describe your activity or business in a particular way?

Many creatives I've taught have found this to be an effective way to begin. It's a vision of your end goal that will constantly motivate and inspire you. Use this imaginary conversation across many scenarios to identify the things you need and the steps you will take to make your goal a reality.

SHARED EXPERIENCE

I asked my coaching client Paige Stevens Holsapple from the USA to complete this task and here's what we dreamed up:

The scenario: As a consumer of my target market, Joanne (Rachael) was asking Susie (me), "Have you heard about a new designer who has a line called Republic of Nostalgia? What do you think about incorporating some of her New Heritage designs in our weekend retreat?"

Joanne said, "I like the vintage vibe, yet bursts of color—that would lend an updated feel for sure."

Susie agreed, "The pieces I've seen would be great and the stories behind them would bring added interest to our rustic setting." Joanne added, "Well, lucky for Paige, I've got ten million pounds to spend!"

After this conversation Paige found that her brand identity became a lot clearer. I then advised her to get all the pieces in place to reflect this. If she wanted her brand to have a retro, vintage yet modern feel, then her website, social media, and portfolio would all need to show this in order to attract this kind of consumer.

KEY ADJECTIVES

Another thing I often do is write key adjectives on little pieces of paper and I use them to influence promotion, press biographies, and the core values for my creative work.

Consider that when people come to you, whether it's your website, or your Instagram, do they get a feel for you? Do they know what colors typically relate to you? Are you someone who's playful? Are you someone who's more sophisticated? Is that message coming across? Are you using the right language when describing your products or your services? Are you putting the right message out there so that people understand instantly what you're about?

You have the power to curate how you're perceived through confident and strong descriptions. For example, early on in my career I really spent time working on captions for imagery, a detailed biography, and a key word list that would help identify my brand.

When I was featured in various press, I was never surprised by how they described me, as more often than not, it was almost identical to the resources they had researched.

Think about your key words for everything you do, from emails to promotional PDFs. The creativity with our words is just as important as our art. When it comes to shaping how we're perceived, it can feel daunting and a lot of people tend to get hung up on this feeling like there's pressure to be the perfect package. My advice is to always stay true to your authentic self and the rest will come that much easier.

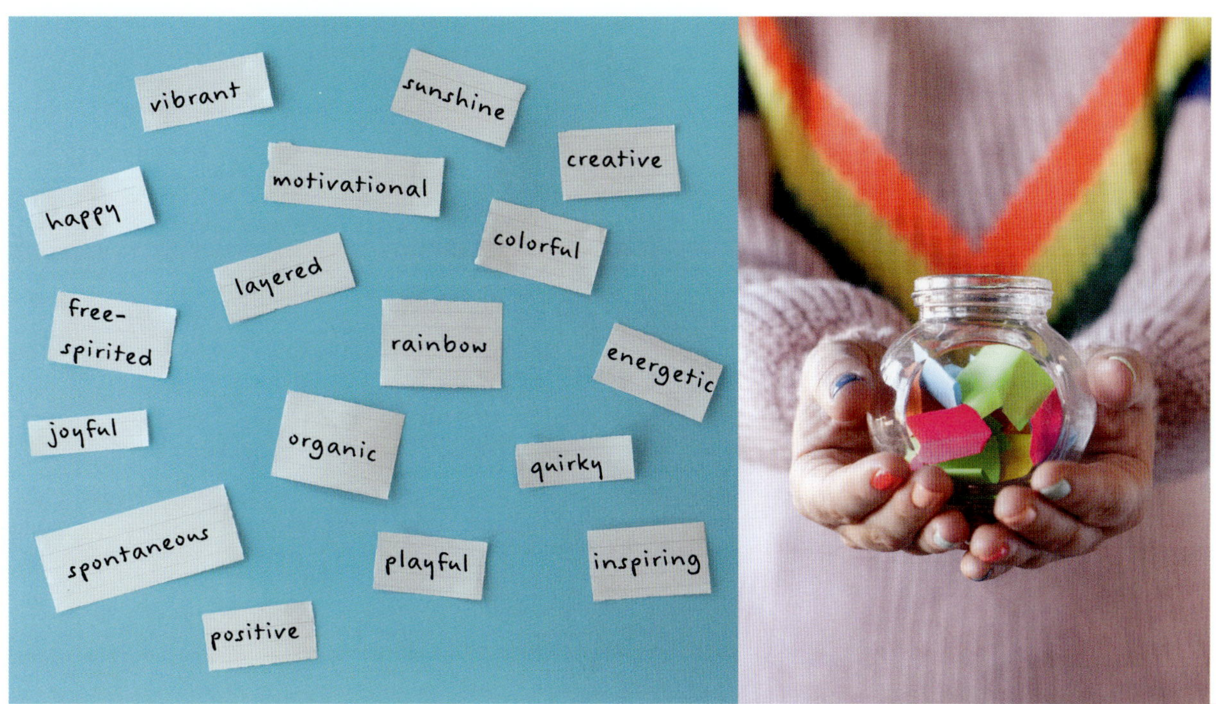

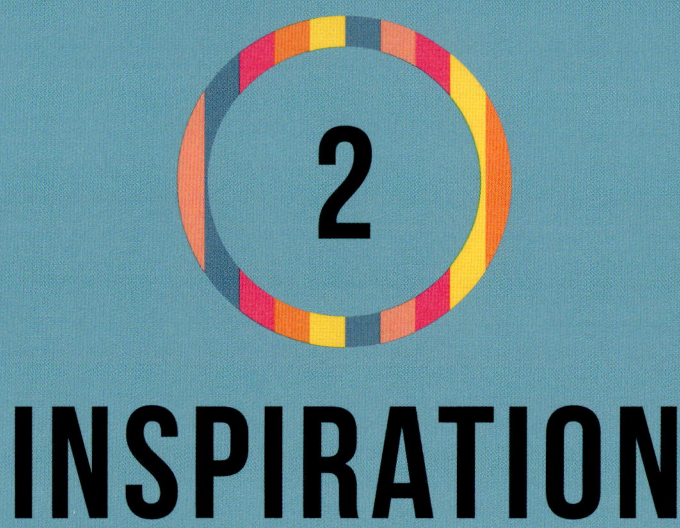

INSPIRATION

How do I become and stay inspired?

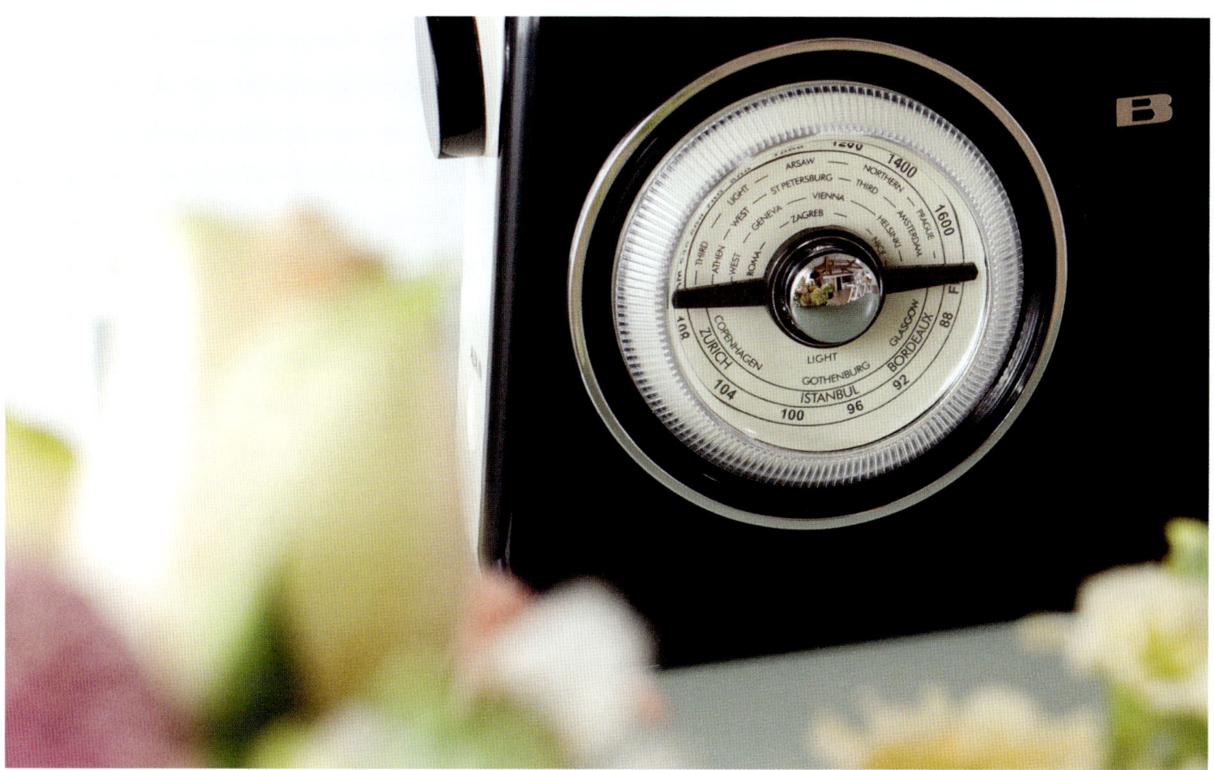

Part of the gift of creativity is that we can see inspiration all around us when we open our eyes, minds, and souls to it. I personally think that inspiration can sometimes feel like a dial in my brain that is constantly on and turned up to 12, but during times of stress it's at 0. Knowing how to effectively keep that dial at 12, and in a way that isn't distracting or overwhelming, is something that takes practice.

I want to guide you on how to use your unique gift in a way that will enrich your life and career. I want to show you how to seek inspiration and get creative, and I will talk you through how to use your inner magic and inspiration to get you through any difficult times.

Sometimes I find myself in a completely noncreative mood or actually a damn right bad or odd mood in general! It can be linked to something obvious, such as stress, upset, or tiredness, and at times it can run much deeper. However, a lot of times I can just be in a bit of a funk. I feel like my mojo has left me to go on vacation and refuses to return until I have a word with myself and figure it out.

As I've matured, I've come to recognize mood changes and realize that there will always be ebbs and flows to my creativity and inspiration, and that's just the way of life.

THOUGHTS TO PONDER ON INSPIRATION

Over many years through Make It In Design I've helped thousands of creatives from all around the world chase their dreams, make bold moves, find inspiration, and discover ways to pull themselves out of a creative rut. Not only do I need to keep myself from going down that dark rabbit hole, but I want to keep many creatives motivated too.

One thing I have learned from my teaching and creative experiences is that you do need to let yourself feel all the feels to be able to find inspiration, whether it's happiness, sadness, anger, frustration, boredom, or excitement. This is human nature, and our feelings need to be expressed to be our true creative selves. However, as important as it is to get the emotion out, we also might need help knowing how to move on, snap out of it, and become more resilient.

When I find myself feeling really low, I'll ride it out, take a slow day, let the emotions surface, and trust in knowing that the balance will be restored again. Without going into too much detail, I have suffered with depression and I'm a suicide survivor and that tends to be a shock to many because of my general sunny disposition. I'm by no means a mental health expert, but having firsthand experience of some tough ordeals in my life I can write this with unfiltered honesty and vulnerability. I've always wanted to highlight my own experiences to break the stigma; however, times are changing in our society, with more open discussions about mental health and it's a promising start. If you suffer with mental health issues, it by no means defines whether you are a positive or negative person. I would describe myself as an optimistic, energetic, and positive person who just so happens to have suffered with mental health problems.

We all travel through life experiencing a broad spectrum of feelings and when we go through a storm or a dark time, the anticipation of the good times gives us hope and purpose. All of our other experiences make the happiness we ultimately receive feel that much more euphoric.

I wanted to share some personal insight around losing your creative spark and how to get it back, along with practices that have been successful for me and my community. How can we use all our emotions to fuel our creativity? They are resources we can tap into just like anything else.

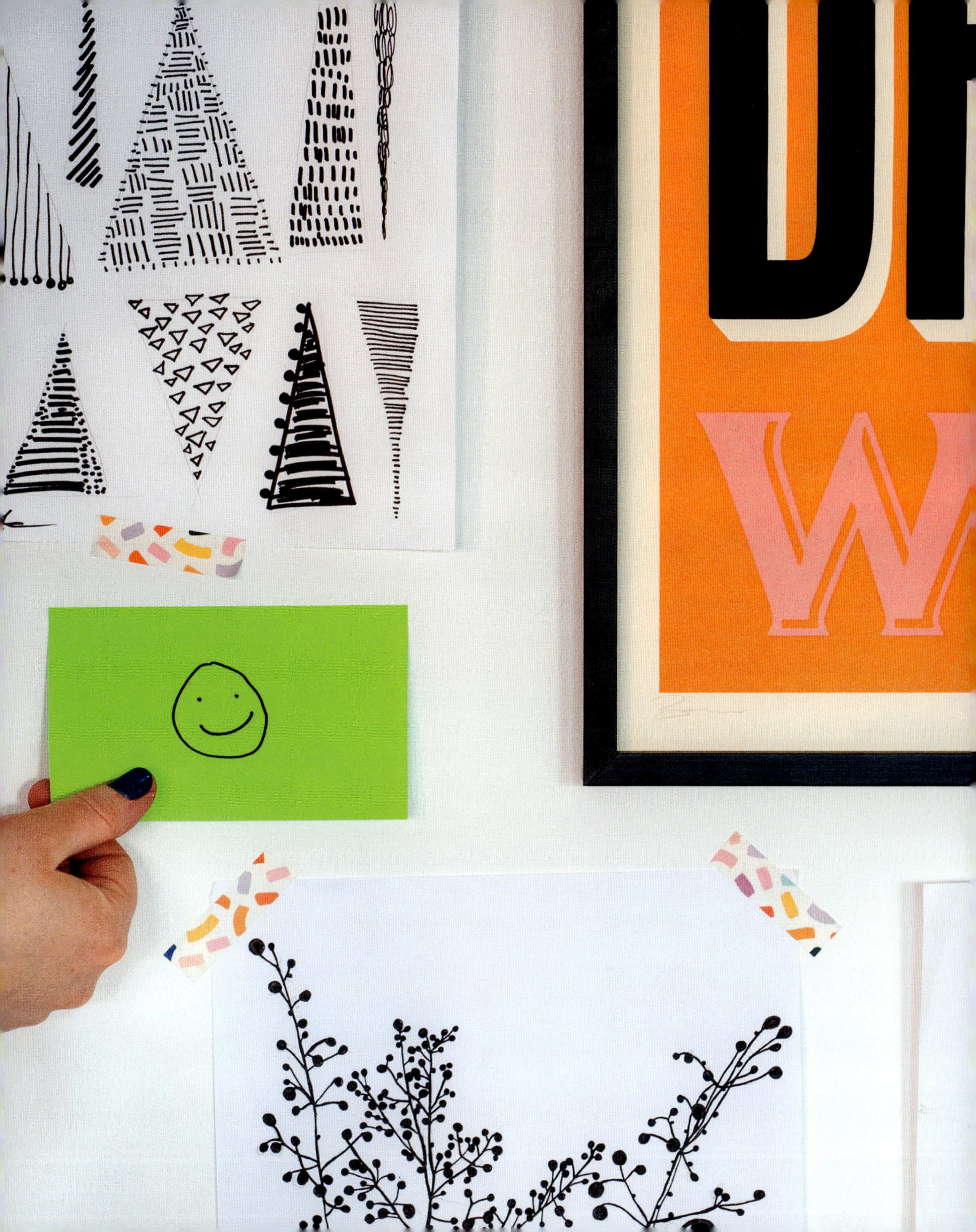

CREATIVE EXERCISES

GETTING OUT OF A FUNK AND FINDING INSPIRATION IN STRESSFUL TIMES

When you think of happiness and what inspires you creatively, what are the top five things that come to your mind? For me it's:

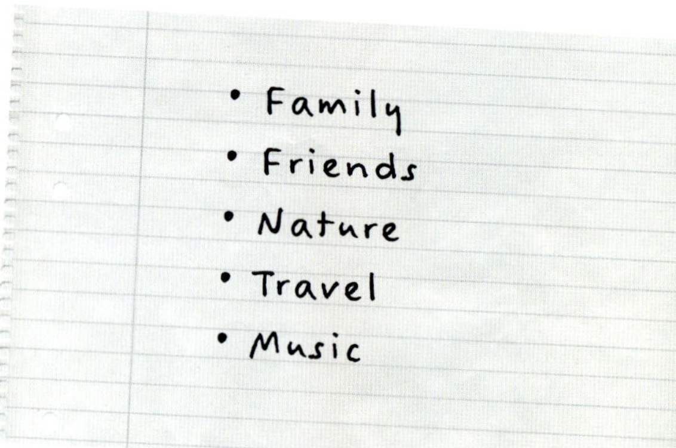

These are the ingredients that keep me cooking and keep up my creative energy, and I often come back to this list when I'm stuck and wonder how I can implement these in my life more.

If I'm on a deadline and time is against me, I'll tweak little things, such as change up my playlist, pop some yummy treats on my desk, call my mum, or switch my desktop screensaver to a cherished travel memory. Honestly, it works wonders! Sometimes it's an instant boost, other times it can take hours, but subconsciously my mind is being filled with those happy ingredients or my senses are being heightened by the sound of my favorite song or the smell of freshly baked cookies.

Whether you are working from your bed on your laptop, on a corner of your busy dining room table, in a coffee shop, or on the move, there is inspiration to be found that can improve your situation and your mental well-being. Ultimately bringing results and ending that stuck-in-a-rut feeling, allowing you to maximize your creative potential.

I'd also like to highlight that I have created some great art while in a less than stellar mood. Even when feeling frustrated in the process, you can still create art when you feel upset or angry. Why not own the feeling and inject it into your art? In return you just may soothe the uneasy feelings away. Creativity can become your medicine.

However, most of the time when I create art, I like to make sure I'm in the right frame of mind, and I've always been told people can feel the joy and energy in my designs. After chatting with my peers and community, many agree they work best when they feel happy, inspired, or motivated.

It's also important to continually remind yourself why you're doing what you're doing creatively. Ask yourself the following questions any time you're having a wobble, and answer honestly, even if you don't like the answer.

Just keep reminding yourself why you are doing these things; if you find you don't like the answers, then it may be time to find some new inspiration, change something up, or look at what you are working on from another perspective.

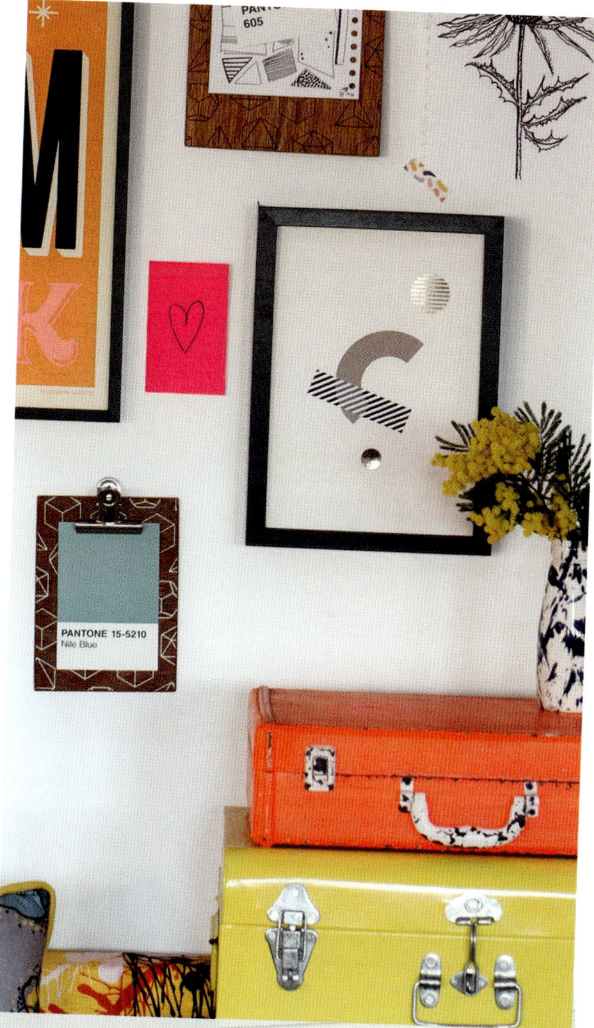

- Why are you really doing what you're doing?
- Why is this thing your dream or goal?
- How does it make you feel right now?
- What is it going to help you achieve?
- Is it going to make you have a better life?
- What impact will it have on your life?
- Is it what you've always wanted?

DISCOVERING INSPIRATION IN OTHERS

Look to those around you for inspiration. There might be a family member or friend who is also creative. Even if they're from a different discipline, the fact that they're following their passions shows that you can do it too. Can you go to a local art or networking event or join an online group? This is why I adore my online community. No matter what time of day or night, there's activity, inspiration, and—most importantly—support.

SHARED EXPERIENCE

My client Sarah Chaudry from New Zealand came to me having doubts whether her work was "good enough," and often this self-doubt can affect the flow of inspiration.

"Having that second voice is so powerful because it reaffirmed my desire to keep going for my design dreams. It was lovely to reconnect to my creative side that I had neglected for so long and made me feel alive again. What's the point in not using your gifts?

After speaking with Rachael I felt inspired to keep taking steps toward my dreams, no matter how small. I recently finished my website, which I'm really happy with, and I now feel confident to approach potential new clients.

This was the first time I had ever spoken to a professional designer about my work, and by doing so it made my dream feel more real and attainable."

Cheer each other on.

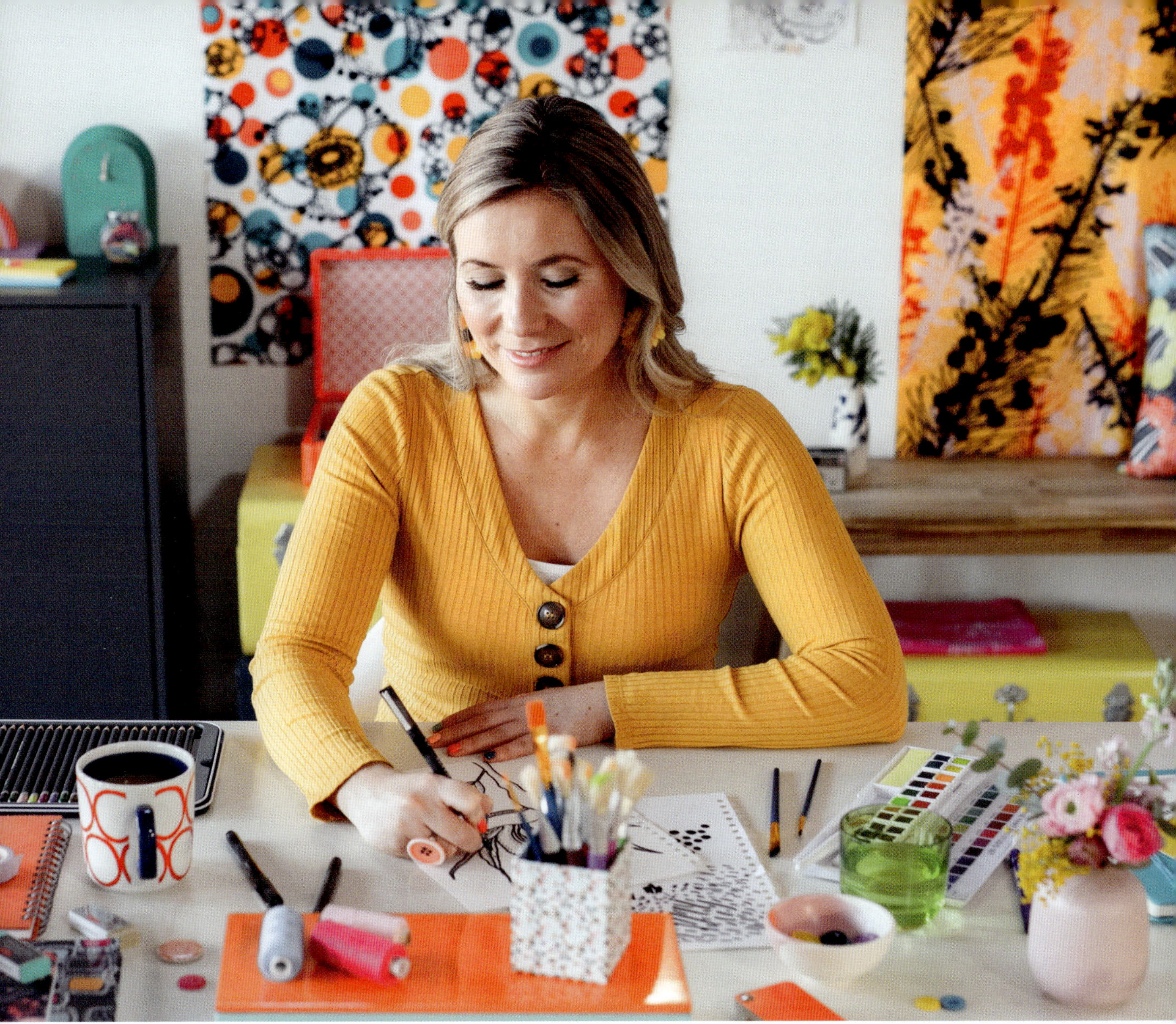

Take some time to look at people you admire, and don't feel intimidated. They may be a lot further along on their journey, but everyone started somewhere. Let them inspire you. What is it that makes you go to their website? What makes you love their Instagram account when their image pops up on the feed? Do they share inspiring quotes? Is it just that you absolutely adore their products? Do you love their photography style? Have a think about that and use it to really inspire you when you're looking at all of your own creative offerings.

CREATIVE DIRECTION CHALLENGES

My job can require a large amount of screen time, and if there's miserable weather outside, my creative spark feels incredibly flat. There have been moments when I don't want to even pick up a drawing pen. These are the times when I need steering in a clear direction and an injection of something fun to work on.

A task that has proven to be really effective in my community is our #7daychallenges that we visually curate and post online. Life might be hectic for you; you may be up against deadlines, trying to look after children or relatives, and you're feeling lost or uninspired.

This is when a set theme, challenge, or schedule that you can fully commit to can drive your way creatively forward. Even if you feel you don't have the time, you can, and will, find a way to make the time if you want to nourish your creative skills and do something for YOU. Unrestrictive inspiration that has purpose inspires me to break free and follow my intuition, and this way of thinking can indirectly become the catalyst for an array of new, highly energized personal pieces.

There are plenty of challenges online specially curated for creatives to dive into, many of which are available on Instagram. Some examples include:

#inktober
#dailyart
#30daysartchallenge
#365daysofart
#100dayproject
#100daychallenge
#colormyeveryday
#thesketchbookproject

You can spend two minutes on a simple doodle or two hours starting a masterpiece—the choice is yours. Try to embrace it creatively, having fun rather than seeing it as a chore.

A drawing a day might excite you, but equally you might feel scared or overwhelmed by that thought. Simply pick and choose what you want to do from this guide, and you can always adapt these creative exercises to fit around your needs.

To start, try a simple seven-day floral drawing challenge:

Day 1 - Daisy
Day 2 - Jasmine
Day 3 - Tulip
Day 4 - Lupin
Day 5 - Cow Parsley
Day 6 - Blanket Flower
Day 7 - Mimosa

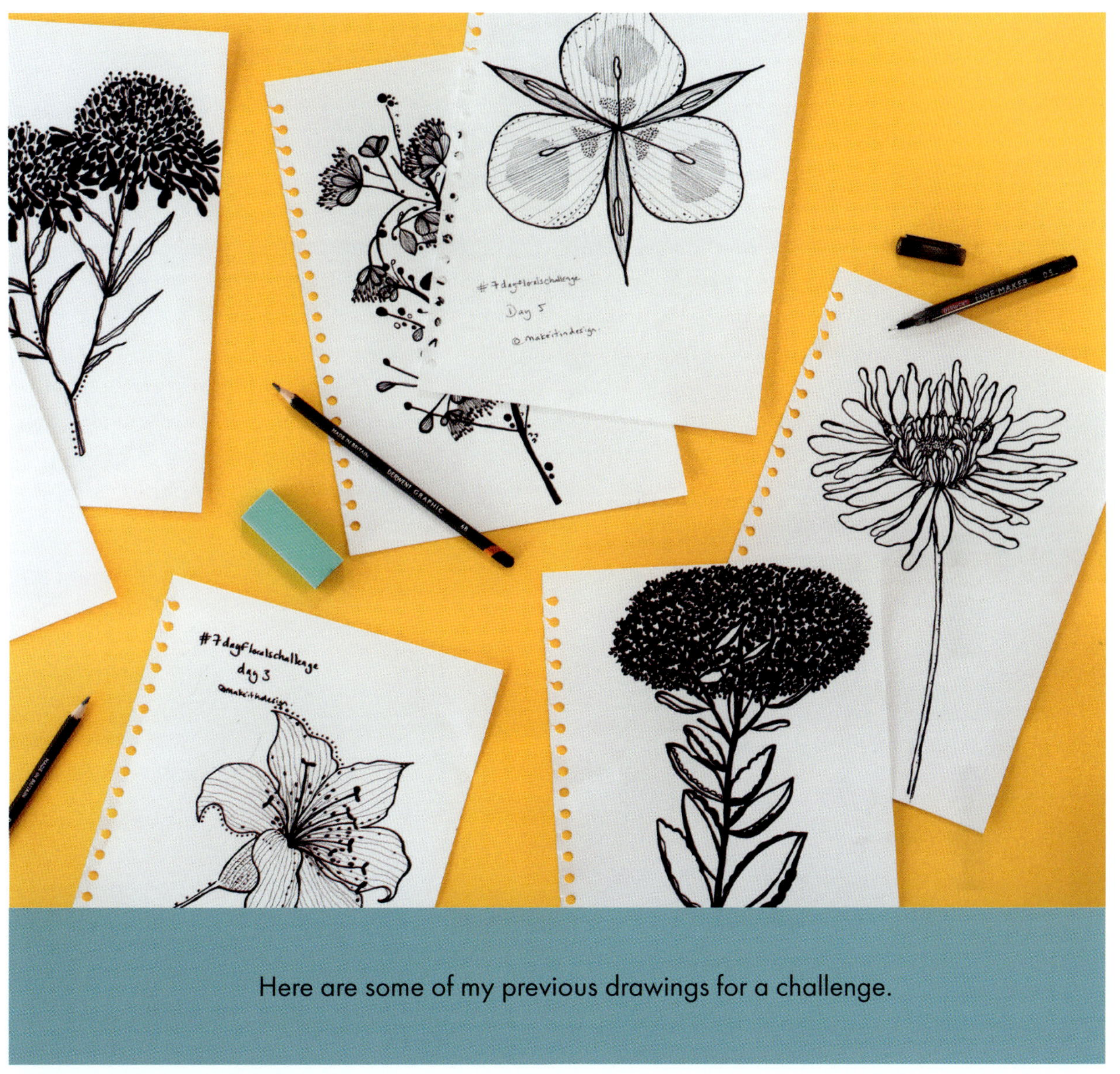

Here are some of my previous drawings for a challenge.

You can either draw a single item or create a grouping, they can be representational or abstract, delicate or bold, fully formed or a quick doodle. Remember to play to your own strengths. For example, if abstract art is your jam, then start creating your response in an abstract way and ease yourself into the project. You can always challenge yourself later down the line by trying new methods when you feel the weight of any negative feelings lifting.

FINDING THE BEAUTY IN THE EVERYDAY

It's often said that even on our bad days we should look for at least one good thing. I challenge you to look around you, and I mean ***really*** look around you, and soak up the inspiration in your environment, as there really is so much beauty in what can be mundane to us and can easily go unnoticed.

Try closing your eyes and clearing your mind for just a few minutes. When you open them again, think of how a child seeing your room for the first time would react. Would they be inquisitive? Do you think the textures and finishes would grab their attention and make them reach out small hands to touch and feel? Would they find unusual shapes that spark their curiosity and imagination? Do you think that everything would feel so new that it would naturally encourage exploration? Now make a list of what you can see through these innocent, unfiltered eyes.

I challenge you to look beyond what is considered traditional beauty or the typical points of interest and see what you can come up with. You can try this exercise in a variety of places and see where the results take you. For example, in my bedroom I observed:

- The textured wood grain on the frame of my bed—lines, waves, a sense of storytelling through age, part of a journey.
- The quirky handle shapes on my dresser—shiny, unique, ordered.
- The power outlet—it somehow looks like a cheeky face.
- The shadows on the wall cast by the fairy lights—delicate, enticing, beautiful.
- The dappled light streaming through my window—soft, calming, luxurious.

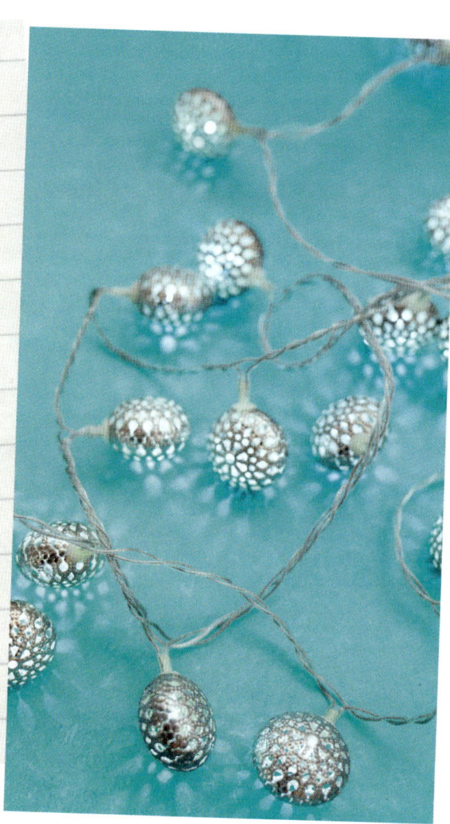

- An eclectic array of makeup brushes—colorful, striking, fluffy, soft.
- Varied sizes and unique styles of perfume bottles—quirky, fun, elegant, sophisticated.
- Clothes hangers—curved, smooth, silhouette, structure.
- Silhouettes of houseplants—structured, busy, intertwined.

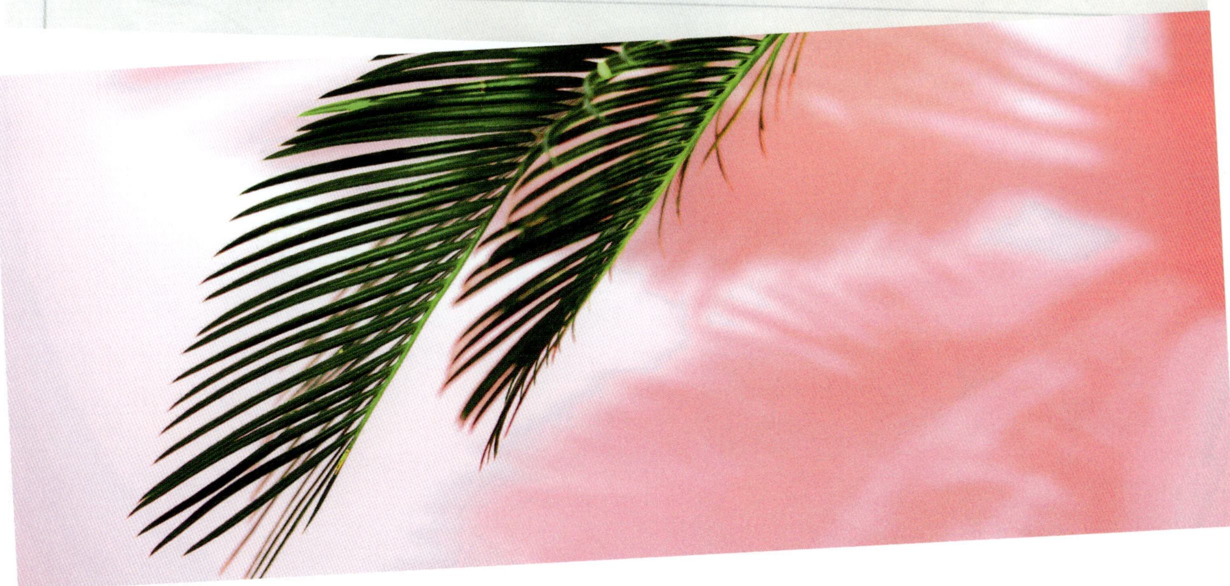

Just from completing this simple task, taking some brief notes, and observing all of the inspiration around me, I have embraced a welcome distraction, felt inspired, and heightened my sense of curiosity to explore my creativity more. I now want to actively do something with the new ideas whirling around in my head. Whether I take action right away or they're left in my subconscious, it doesn't really matter, as they provided a creative escape and have opened my creativity to many more possibilities.

THE JOY OF MULTITASKING

Like many, I found myself unexpectedly having to homeschool during the Covid-19 pandemic and I had to juggle many life commitments, a full-time creative job, and two businesses. I experienced all of the emotions from trying to be regimented and have a schedule. In trying to do so, I realized that I had put so much unnecessary pressure on myself thinking I had to give a 110 percent to work, being a mother, and trying to be a teacher—and all with a smile on my face. I'm often told my upbeat energy is infectious, but trust me—there are many days when I'm totally flat.

A few failed banana breads later, I gave in to the fact that some things will go well on certain days and other areas not so much. I just have to do what I need to do to stay afloat. From this experience I've learned to shift my daily focus, recognize my energy level and what mood I'm in, and notice how everyone else is doing.

With this balancing act comes what feels like a restricted window for my creativity, and it makes the dedicated time I do have more precious. Where possible, I continually try to fuel my creativity through my subconscious and multitask. Here are some examples:

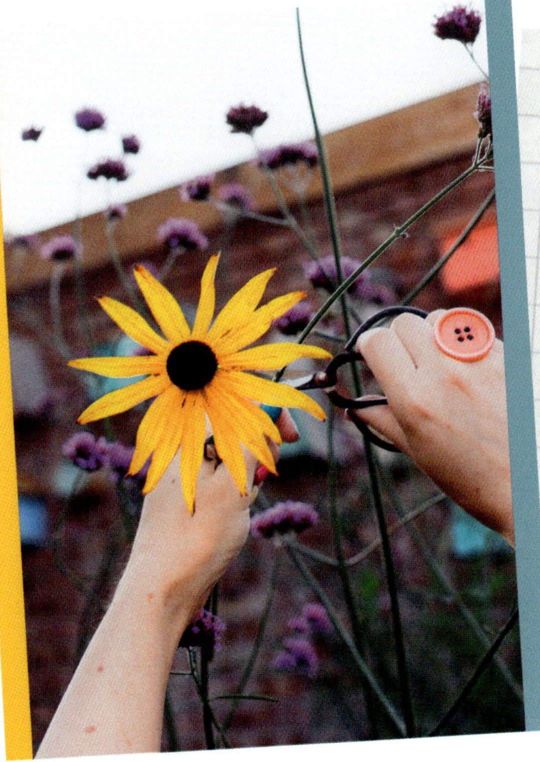

- Chores + music. When I'm cleaning I'll also listen to my favorite music.
- Gardening + photography. When I'm outdoors, I'll also take my phone and capture the beauty that I see to spark ideas later on.

- Explore + imagine. When I'm with my son we take in everything around us, and I embrace and encourage his curious mind to ask questions.

- Rest + create. If I'm just wanting a rest on the sofa, I'll also aimlessly doodle, not overly thinking, just letting my imagination go where it may.

- Comfort + creativity. I paint my home in colors of the rainbow to change my mood, so that I'm constantly surrounded by inspiration to fuel my creativity.

So with this multitasking idea in mind, playing Pokémon with my son in the house became a Pokémon catching exploration in the woods, jumping on logs, climbing trees, and discovering dens. Alongside playing, we were also getting fresh air and exercise. While this was happening, my subconscious was absorbing the glistening sunlight through the trees, the glorious birdsong, the perfumed aroma of the flowers, the beauty of the shadows, all while blissfully laughing and having fun. In what could have been a stressful time with extra hours to fill, I leaned into the moment, recognized how precious it was to have quality time with Blayke, and the next day my notebook became flooded with new design ideas that were all based on that one unintentional creative walk (and no, they weren't about Pikachu!).

This experience encouraged me to keep going with my important nurturing ingredients daily. No matter how restricted we feel, the little things can add up to big things when it comes to improving our mental health and enriching our creativity.

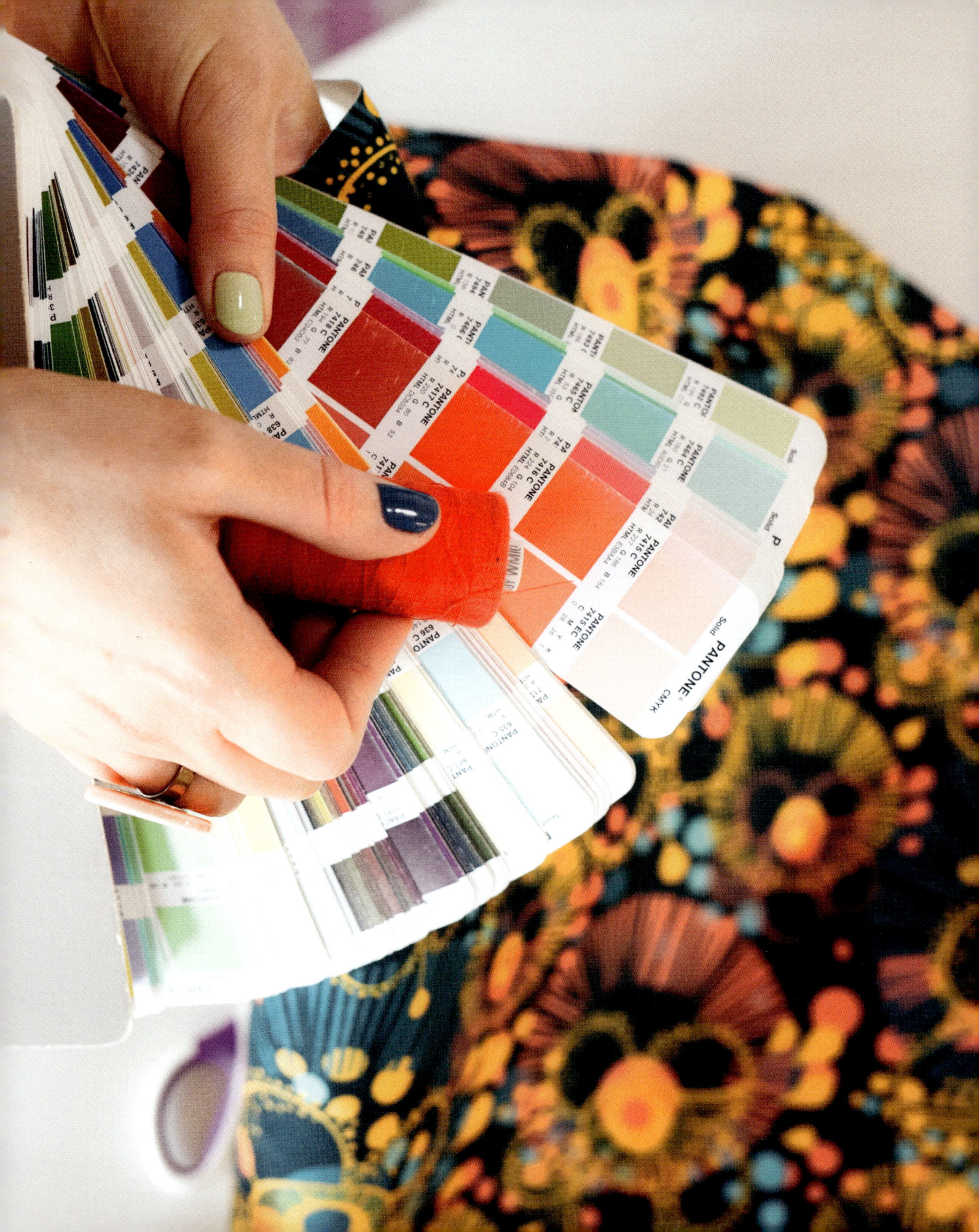
PANTONE 7418 C
PANTONE 7417 C
PANTONE 7416 C
PANTONE 7415 C
PANTONE 7415 EC
Solid
PANTONE
CMYK

EMBRACING COLOR

Our life choices, our daily surroundings, the food we eat, the TV we watch, the books we read, the music we listen to, and the company we keep can impact our creativity so much, and so can color. While color psychology is another book in itself, I want to briefly explain that the colors in your home or office as well as those you wear can impact your mind-set and productivity.

Sure, we're all aware of generic descriptions—red can evoke anger, passion, and warmth, while blue is serene, soothing, and tranquil. However, we all have our favorite colors, and different colors can impact individuals so differently. I personally adore orange, yellow, and coral, which to me represent warmth, sunshine, energy, and feel-good vacation vibes, so I'm generally at my best when I'm around or wearing them. While many might find grays and beige so soothing, they have the opposite effect on me. I find them draining, uninspiring, and boring, and when wearing them or being overly surrounded by them I feel completely flat.

Is the aesthetic that you surround yourself with a tonic to your creativity or something that drains you? Bring in some of your favorite colors as much as you can. You don't always have to paint interiors—it could be bright office accessories, plants and flowers, or the colors you select from your wardrobe. Embrace the joy of what's being called "dopamine dressing"!

If the thought of creating a palette feels overwhelming to you, then grab your favorite top, tablecloth, or scarf and simply use that as a starting point. A popular task with my community is to create a 3D physical color palette that you can use anything for, from your kids' toys to food, clothing, and utensils. Don't be afraid to mix the objects up. I often do this as a bit of light relief on heavy admin days, as it can be a great way to inspire palettes for my artwork and often influences my choice of interiors. Color play is a great form of art therapy and brilliant for powering up your creativity.

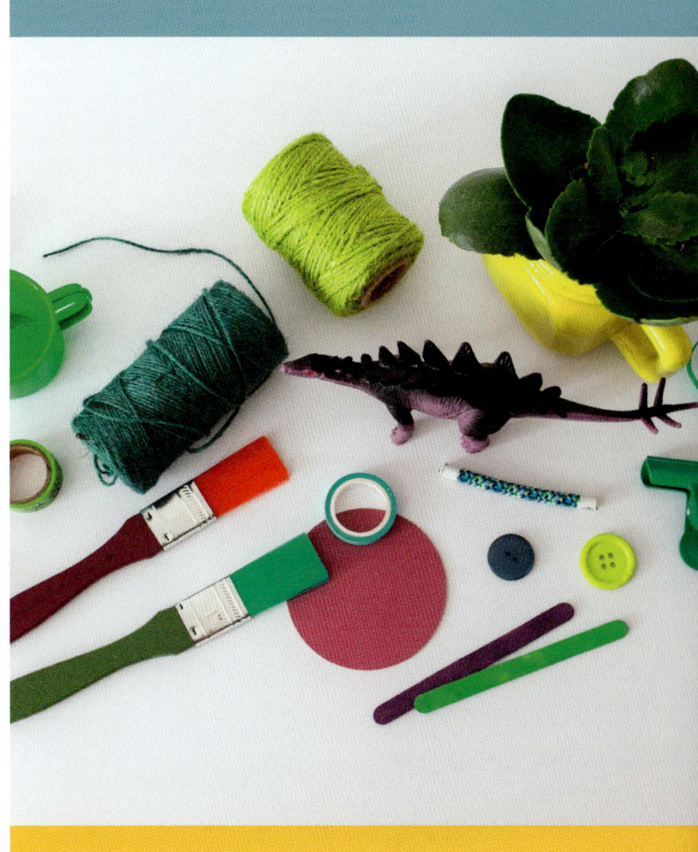

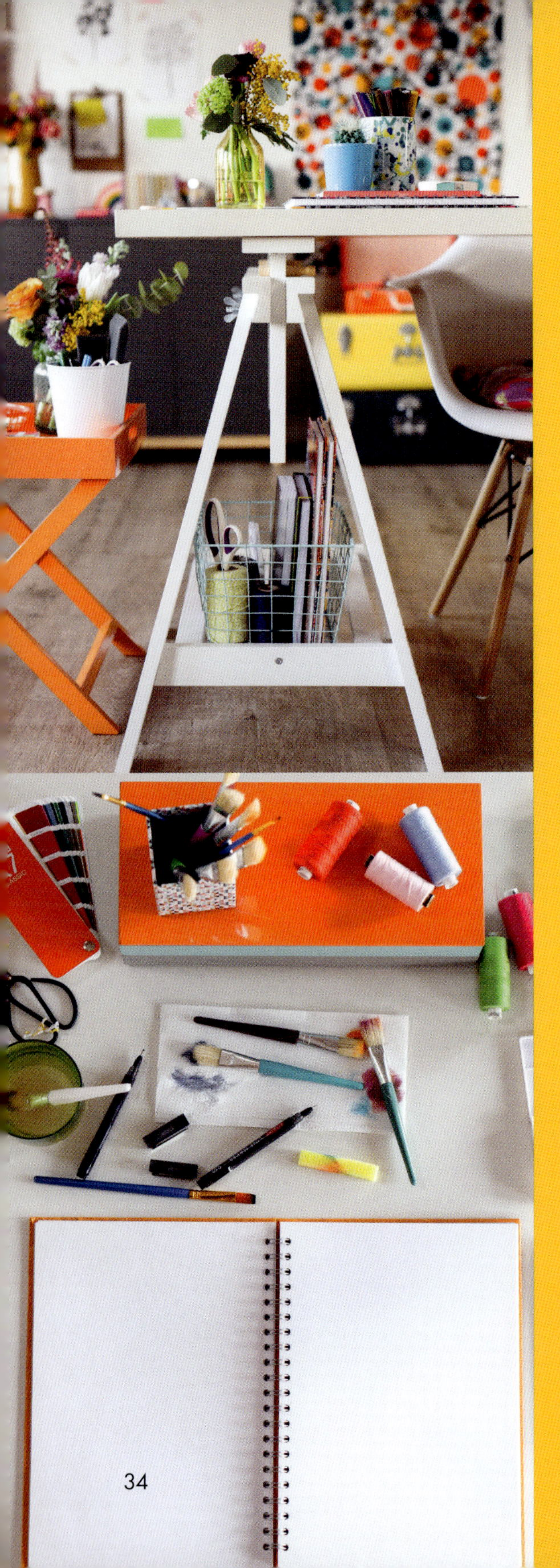

INSPIRING WORKSPACE

Simple things, such as beautifying your space, can make a positive impact.

I absolutely love having fresh flowers dotted about, nice lighting, and sitting by a window if possible. Some of you might be working from a kitchen table, and that's fine as well. I'd like you to think about what you can do to make your space feel more comfortable. What will help you focus and work at your best? Is it sitting on a pretty, comfy pillow? Settling into a tidy workspace or worktable? Having good music on in the background?

When I'm working on more design-based work and at my home studio, I tend to have a little photo on my desk. Right now, I have one of my son Blayke from when he was really young. I look at that and I think, "I'm working hard because I want to achieve my goals for both of us." Whenever I have great success, my son also reaps the rewards, and our life gets a bit easier, so he's definitely my biggest motivation and inspiration. Remind yourself of the value in doing what you're doing and use that as your driving force.

I also encourage you to think about the ambience of your setting. I'm a big fan of candles, essential oils, and decorating with uplifting quotations. Use anything that boosts your excitement and passion and can make your day feel that much more fun. As artistic people, creativity is at the heart of everything that we do, so even when we're just working on admin, we can dress our space to provide inspiration.

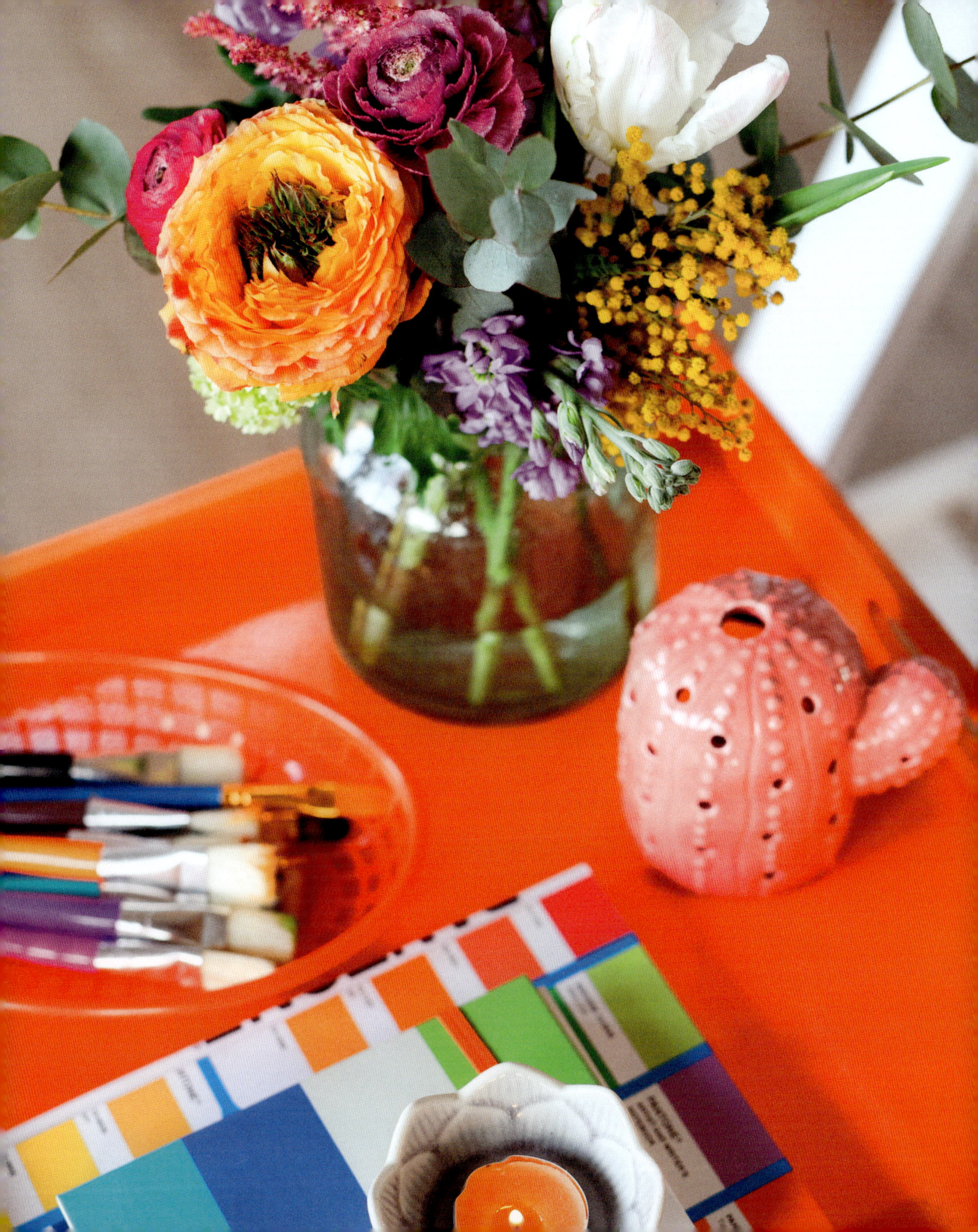

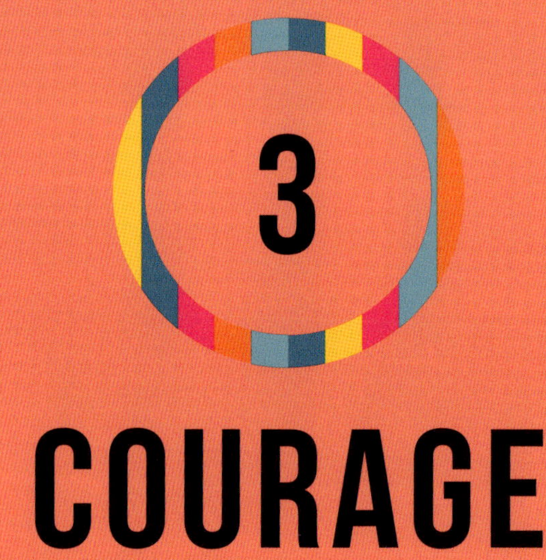

3 COURAGE

What do I need to be creatively courageous?

If it were easy, everyone would do it.

Whenever we try something new or strive for bigger and better things, we are reaching into the unknown. Hard work and preparation can make the transition easier, but it's very rare that something is guaranteed. We must have the ability to do things that scare us and act with bravery to make things happen and give ourselves the courage to dream big.

We can continue to play it safe, and perhaps that's enough to feel content, but as creatives we all know there's so much to explore out there. Life is for living, days are for dreaming, the world is for exploring, and your creativity is there to be celebrated!

I have never really opened up about the struggles I've had in my earlier days—the bullying especially—because it's so emotional to reflect on. For some, it may seem that everything has come together for me seamlessly, but that's not always the case. I could have given up when I was told by bullies I couldn't do it, or when I saw my design in a shop window on the high street used without my permission and felt like one helpless designer against a big corporation, but it only made me stronger as a person and more determined to prove them wrong. My main goal in sharing this is to show you that no matter your struggle, if you stay positive and realistic, work hard, and really follow your instincts (even the risky ones), you too can see your dreams come to fruition.

Trust me when I say even in those dark moments we can shine, and that magic can be created even from the hard stuff. Recognizing when to act and having a positive attitude can take you a long way.

THOUGHTS TO PONDER ON COURAGE

I urge you to aim as high and dream as big as you can, allowing you to expand your creativity to levels more than you have ever imagined. Don't be put off by how long the journey takes. The main thing is you are on that journey, and you won't stop until you reach your desired destination. ***If we dream small, we act small.*** If we don't have a dream so big that it scares us, we never really push ourselves to see what might be on the other side waiting for us.

I try to remind myself it's all "mind over matter" with a lot of things, especially when I'm out of my depth. As Theodore Roosevelt once said, "Believe you can and you're halfway there." Even when we go through tough stuff that's beyond our control or face a setback that derails a plan, we need to remind ourselves that we all have control of how we choose to react to a situation.

Sometimes I remind myself I'm not performing heart surgery and that really puts it all in perspective again. We should always strive for the courage to enjoy our work and, most importantly, never feel guilty or apologize for it.

In this book we talk about the importance of manifesting your dreams and visualization, but right now I ask that you learn to believe in yourself. Look in the mirror and say out loud, "I can do it" or "I've got this." Believe in your creativity; it's your gift to share with others, make your mark, stand tall, and be proud of who you are today. Don't get caught up in the "I'll be happy when X happens" or "I'll feel proud when Y happens." Be proud now.

As creatives, we gain so much enjoyment from the process, from painting a canvas to taking that wonderfully timed photograph. Sure, we love the finished piece, but remember to celebrate having the courage to make that first step.

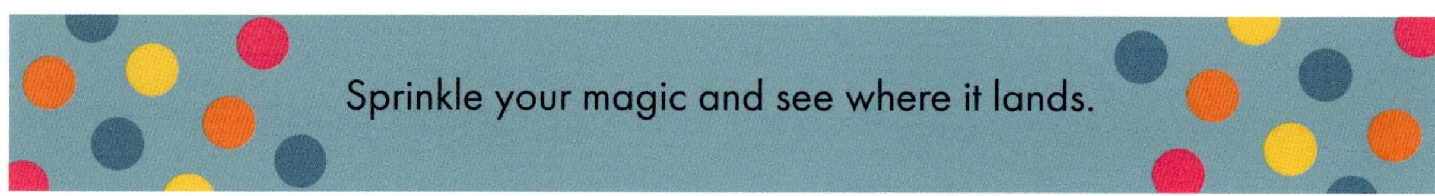

CREATIVE EXERCISES

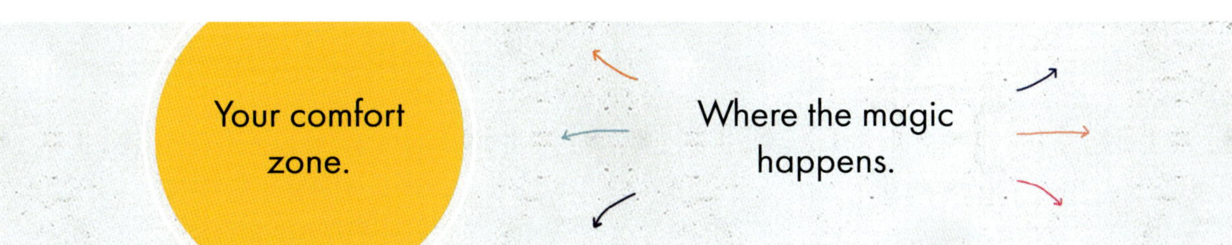

STEPPING OUTSIDE YOUR COMFORT ZONE

I have been pushing myself way out of my comfort zone and it led to me writing this very book. I know how magical an opportunity it is and the new exciting possibilities it can bring. I'm a designer who just so happens to write, so it's not something that is a natural process for me, but creativity is my passion and I'm pretty excited that you are here reading this!

Sitting down and writing used to make me squirm and my procrastination levels would hit the roof, alongside the added problem of my fridge and cupboards being empty from the endless snacks I'd consume. However, the more I wrote, the easier it became. I found short sharp bursts such as Instagram posts, blog captions, or Q&A-style interviews the easiest at first, then I slowly built it up from there. Over time I became more focused and reminded myself that I need to make my audience engaged and stimulated. There was an aha! moment and I realized I manage this well within my design work, so why should this project be any different? Once I adopted that mind-set, I quieted the voices in my head and started to see my keyboard as another tool for self-expression, the same way as I would a drawing pen or paintbrush. I now treat words with as much consideration as selecting the right type of motif or the appropriate colors to convey a message in one of my designs. This has entirely shifted my approach to new projects, and something that was unfamiliar territory now starts to feel familiar and more enjoyable.

NOT GIVING UP

I'd rather look back knowing that I tried, grabbed life with both hands, and gave everything a go. I've made mistakes, I've had failures and been rejected, but I've never given up. In the end, I wouldn't change a thing, as it's brought me to this colorful, creative life that I'm very grateful for. I'm sure there'll be other imperfect situations I'll have to face, and I'm okay with that as long as I keep my passion and continue to power up my creativity.

I think when we're looking out there at people we admire, they've all been through tough things as well. I don't know a successful person who hasn't had a tough experience. The fact is, they don't give up. Or they go on to the next idea and pursue their next dream. As time goes on, you learn from experiences, you grow, and it enriches your life for the better. The more we do things, the more we're trying things, and the more we go after our dreams, the more we become fearless.

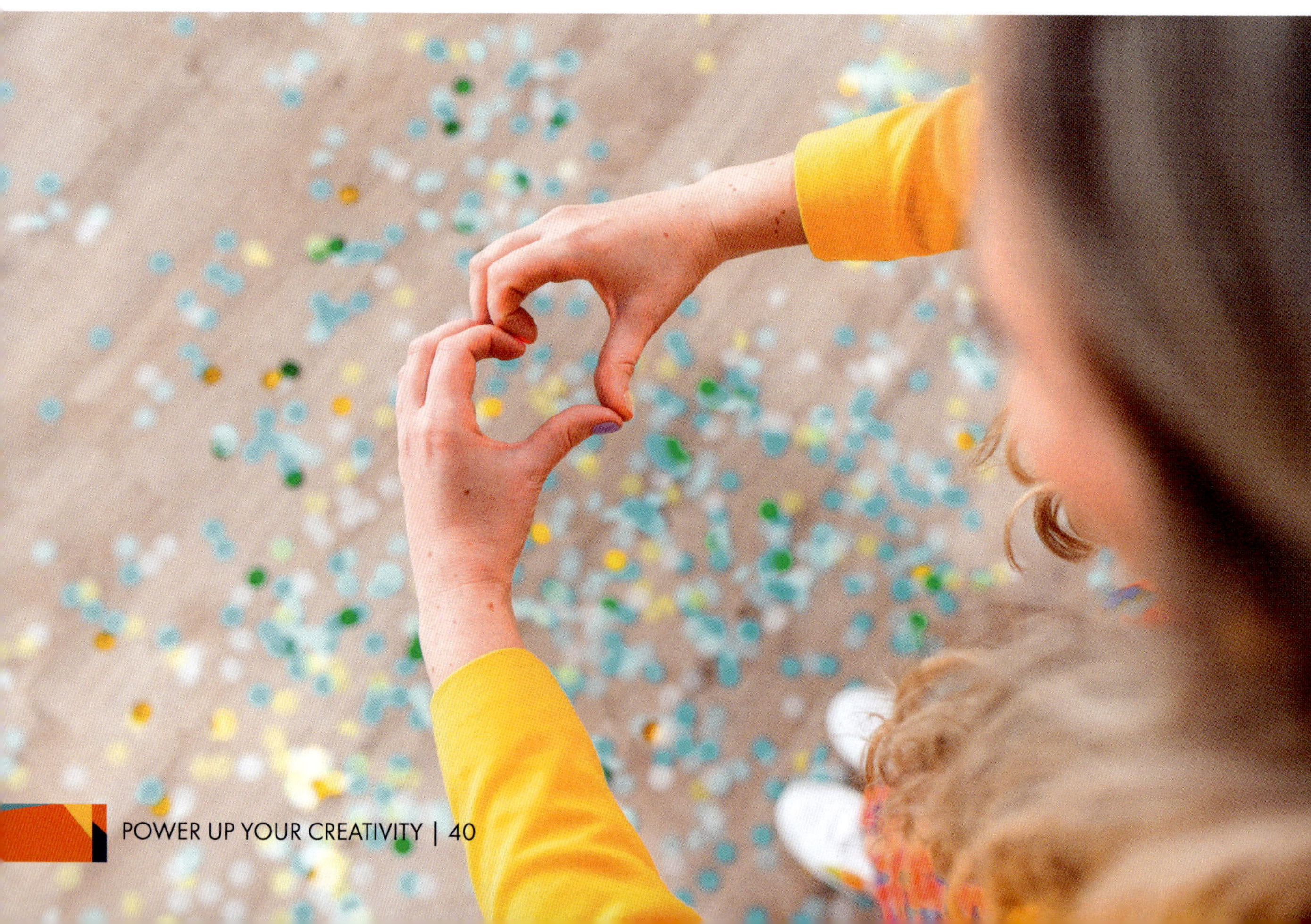

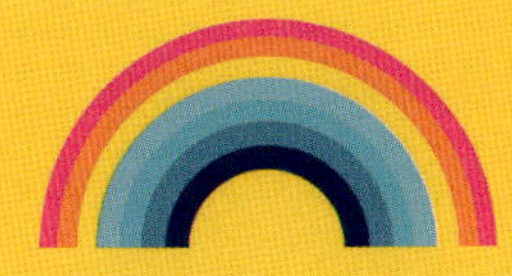

You have to commit to your dreams.

This little saying is so true, and I find the harder I work, the more luck I seem to have. I'm always told, "You're so lucky," "You have a job that's easy," "You get to do what you love." What I can tell you is that I'm so grateful, but it's genuinely not easy being a business owner (and I have two companies that I built from scratch). I don't actually get to design every day or sit among the flowers as some folks think. I have a lot of management duties and responsibilities and pressure, but what I can say is, it's all so worth it in the end!

For those who say my job looks easy, these comments can really frustrate me because as a creative person with a lot of artistic tasks, it doesn't mean I work any less or that I'm less dedicated than someone who works in an office. In fact, there have been many occasions where I've had sleepless nights and tears and worked so many extra hours to deal with overseas clients that I've sacrificed personal time and a social life. It's been a hard slog over the years with the Rachael Taylor Studio and Make It In Design, and there have been many ups and downs, but I wouldn't change a thing.

I started my businesses fairly young with pretty much zero money in the bank. For those wondering about starting a business: If you have enough passion, drive, and determination you can make it happen—but things don't just land on your lap. There have been times I've had deals come in unexpectedly, but they happened because I'd already put in years of groundwork. Having my own creative business is a roller coaster, but I'm here for the long ride.

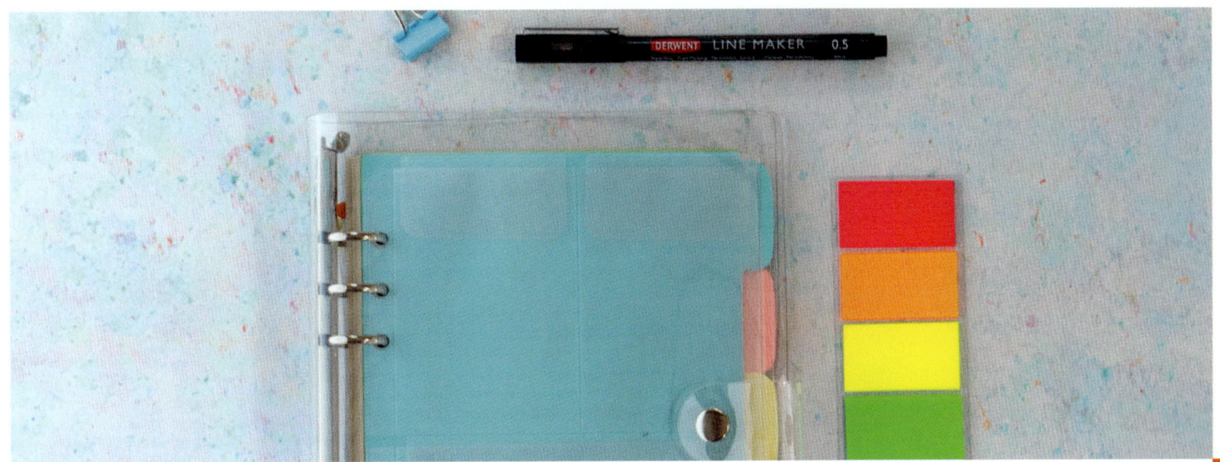

REJECTION IS REDIRECTION

I feel that rejection is often about timing, and that being rejected isn't always about anything ***I've*** done. For example, I reached out to a design agency early on in my career, probably quite naively, and although I felt ready, they said the timing wasn't right. In that moment, it felt awful, but years down the line, they then approached ***me***, and that was amazing. When I got that no, I followed other opportunities and eventually got signed with an even better agency.

So sometimes rejection is a step toward redirection—maybe that sounds cheesy—but I do believe in that. Sometimes things happen for a reason. Sometimes that's nonsense and nothing comes of it, but I think nine times out of ten you're directed to better things. You become more driven once you've had a "no," and after you've gotten over that initial "this feels completely awful" reaction.

However, I've had many other instances with rejection. When I was just starting out, I sent my colorful design collections to British High Street stores and they said, "You're not for us. Your style isn't suited to the UK." It felt horrible at the time, but I didn't give up. I thought, *I know I've got something different to offer here.* I then approached people overseas in the Australian and American markets, and ultimately, I had bigger growth there because they liked all the color.

So that early rejection was actually the best thing that could have happened because it pushed me to develop an overseas audience. Then years later, when trends moved on, I succeeded in the British market. From then on, I've just always been true to myself—one of the key factors that has kept my career flourishing.

Sometimes you can feel rejected in other ways, even if it's not an obvious creative step. Where you get the vibe that people do not like you or your qualities. They might not agree or judge the way you approach things. In this instance, the path for redirection might not always feel clear at the time, but know that life has a funny way of presenting things that eventually make you stronger. This has happened to me multiple times over the years and has been tough. I have to accept the fact that not everyone will like me and that's okay. The more these things happen the more equipped I am to deal with them in the future. At times like this I think of this quote from my friend Mister Fred: "I stop trying to explain myself to those who cannot hear my explanation." Knowing when to walk away is powerful. If something in genuinely making you miserable and affecting your mental health or your body, listen to those signs. Prioritize ***YOU***.

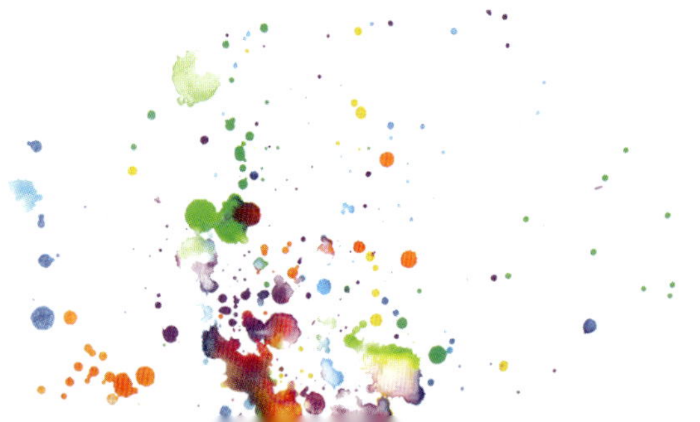

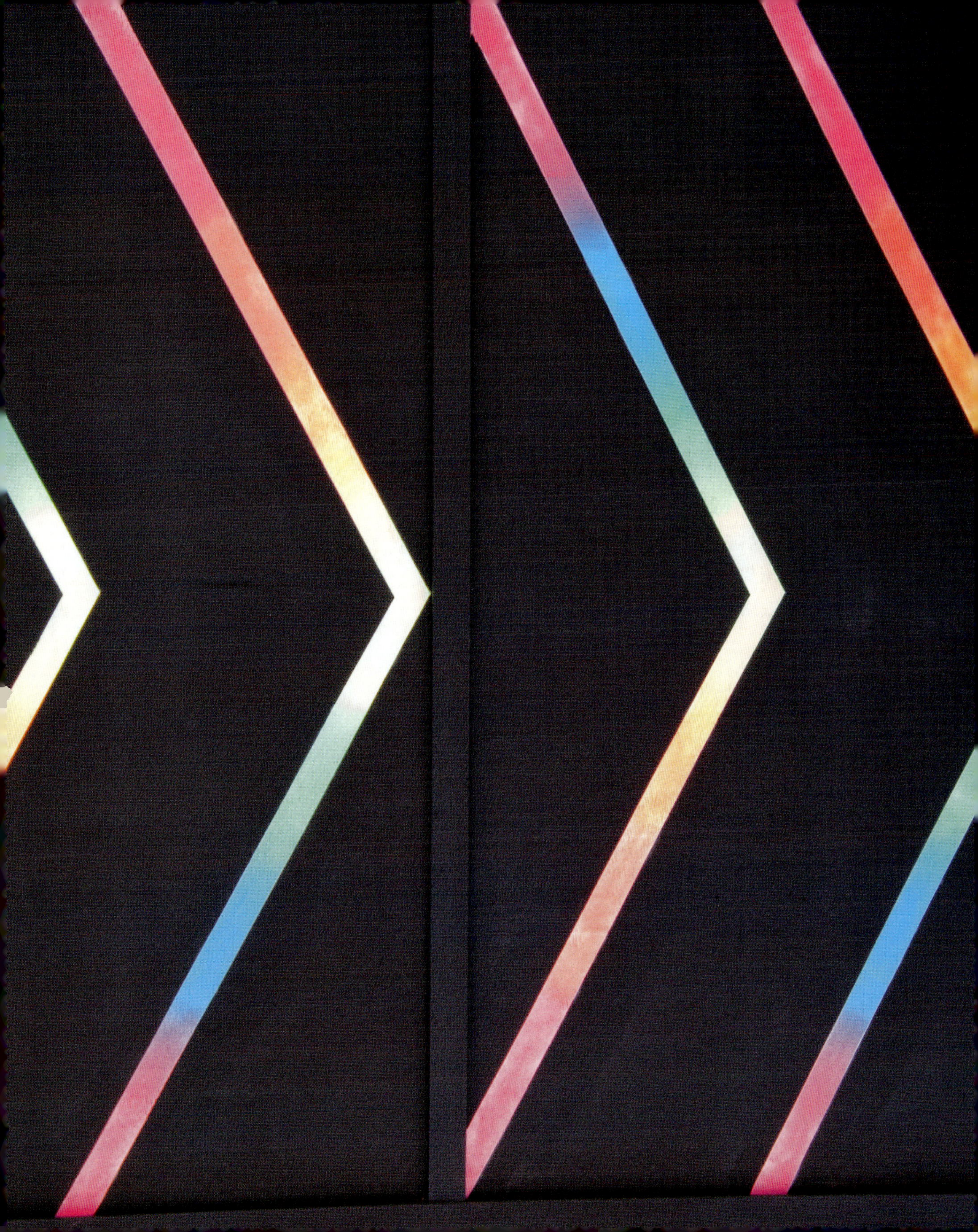

THE COMPARISON DEMON

In moments of upset or stress, many of us spend hours on technology, aimlessly scrolling in the pursuit of a numbing distraction. We all know too well this can be incredibly harmful and counterproductive, and we can't help but compare ourselves to others. It's human nature, and the worst time to do it is when you're not feeling yourself or emotions are running high. There are a number of well-known quotes that I love, such as "Comparison is the thief of joy" by Theodore Roosevelt. By all means look to the people you admire, but understand that you may be at different points in your journey. And it's very much your own personal journey. It's fun and can be inspiring to see what other people are doing, but it's also important to set your own goals and listen to your intuition rather than doing things just because other people are. Don't feel you have to be dragged into an area that everyone else is in, and stay true to yourself—that's how you'll create your own personal style that's uniquely yours.

That person who you think grabs all the deals and seems to get everything—don't give in to jealousy, as actually they're showing you that it's a possibility. Their success was once a dream, something they pondered and then made happen. Things to try when you find the comparison demon strikes:

- ***A digital detox.*** Just stop scrolling, put it down, close it, or switch it off.
- ***Unfollow accounts that make you feel flat or inadequate.*** I'm not saying unfollow accounts of people you genuinely admire here, but ask yourself: Do they make you feel good? Do they stimulate you creatively? Or do they share humor and make you laugh? Or perhaps offer a moment of calm at the end of a hectic day?
- ***Use admiration to drive you and ignite your passion.*** If you see someone doing well or achieving a goal you dream of, think *good for them*, because it shows it can be done. Use that to motivate you.
- ***Celebrate your wins.*** Remember how far you've come and pat yourself on the back for things you achieve, no matter how big or small they are.
- ***Practice gratitude.*** Despite your troubles, think about any moments that provided light during your day: the birds singing, a yummy lunch, a sketch you completed. Remind yourself of the little things and be present in the moment.

Everyone will go through life at their own pace, and that's okay.

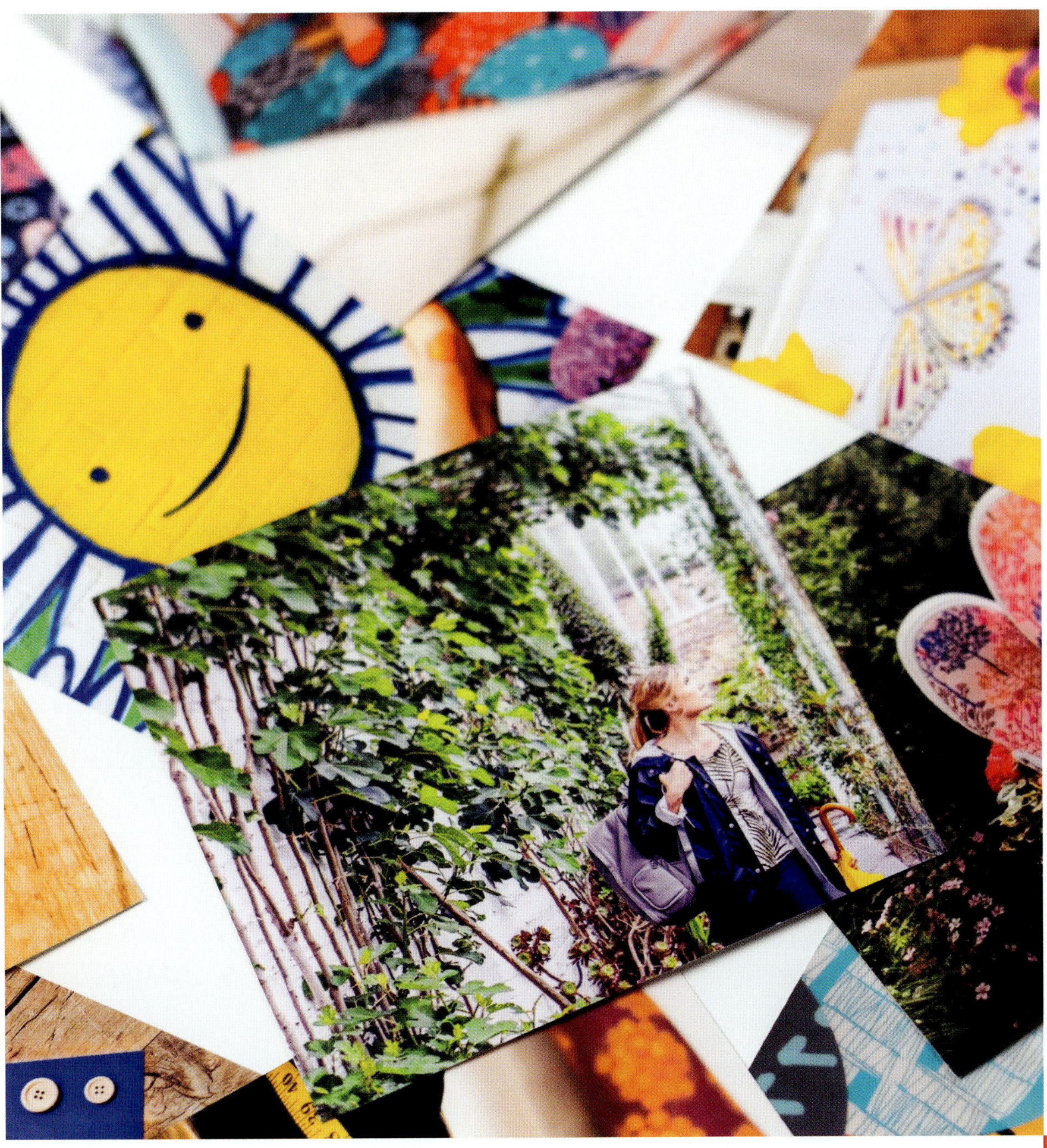

IMPOSTER SYNDROME

Once we've overcome the comparison demon, we can then face imposter syndrome. This is something I personally feel frequently, even while writing this book! You might think it's strange for me to admit this to you, as I'm the one guiding you and cheering you on, but I always like to be transparent and show that you're not alone. Imposter syndrome often strikes when I've secured a dream job, goal, or project. First comes the excitement, the ideas, the process, but once I get stuck in the work, I start to think, "Oh gosh, X company wants this from me, they have such high expectations, what if I can't deliver as I normally do," and then I often have a bit of a wobble.

At times like this, I usually take a breather, go for a walk, attend a yoga class, get coffee with a friend, plan a playdate with my son, or phone my mum, and these things really calm me, ground me, and put things in perspective. Take a few moments and think about or jot down what brings you a sense of calm. Have it at the ready as a tonic for your soul to soothe any of those uneasy feelings as soon as they try to creep in. I also like to remind myself that the company or person chose me for a reason, and that it doesn't matter that my Instagram doesn't look like X, or today I feel a bit scruffy. I need to have faith and confidence in myself to power up my creativity and deliver a great project I know I'm capable of.

Another example would be when I've been hired to speak to a global audience at the likes of the trade show Printsource, New York. Yes, I know on paper I have the experience that ticks all of the boxes for this kind of presentation, yet the thought of it made me squirm. I was younger than the other speakers and worried I wouldn't be taken seriously. I'm also a proud Liverpudlian, and as much as some people can genuinely adore the accent, many mock it or even despise it. When I teach international students I know to speak slower and more clearly, but when I'm nervous I don't control my own speed dial. In the end it went really well, and the audience embraced me with open arms. The qualities that I think people will mock me for are actually the things they find endearing.

So next time that imposter syndrome strikes, remind yourself of how awesome you are!

You deserve all of the good things.

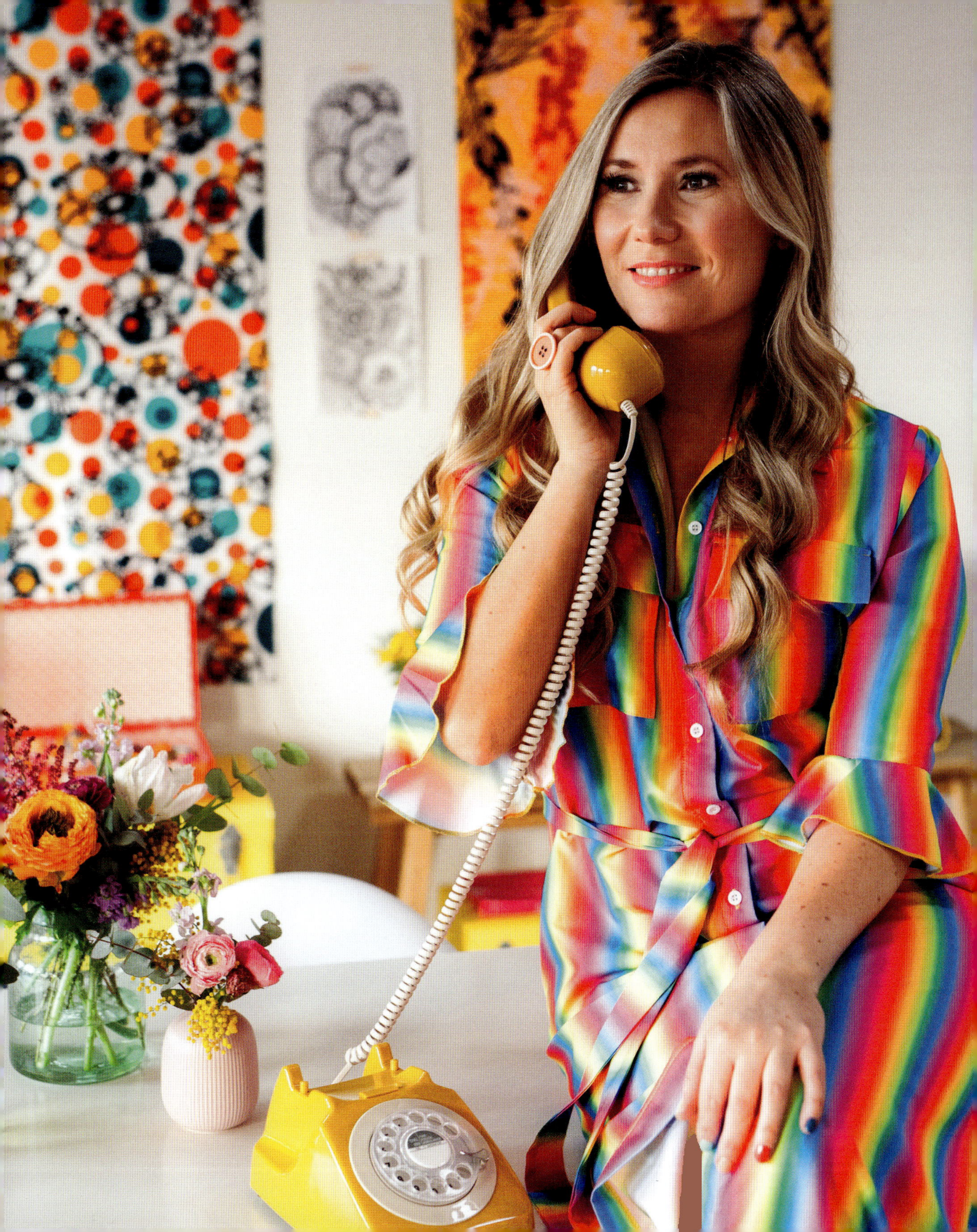

FOLLOW YOUR WEIRD

It's okay to have quirks. Over the years I've come to accept the things that make me weird are the same things that make me my own kind of wonderful.

Without a doubt, my confidence has grown with age, but knowing how to "follow my weird," inject personality into my art, create from the heart, and stay true to my authentic self has brought me longevity in my career.

Sure, there have been times working on a restrictive client brief, or I've been asked to follow a specific trend, or there are budget constraints that put limitations on my unique creativity—in that moment, I can start to feel my confidence slipping. So I take a break, make a cuppa, play my favorite song, and remind myself that the client wants to work with *me*. Over the years I've learned to trust my gut, even when friends and peers might have thought, "What is she doing?" I've embraced my inner weird, and it's opened some magical doors.

I've outlined my weird attributes below and how I feel they can be translated into my art:

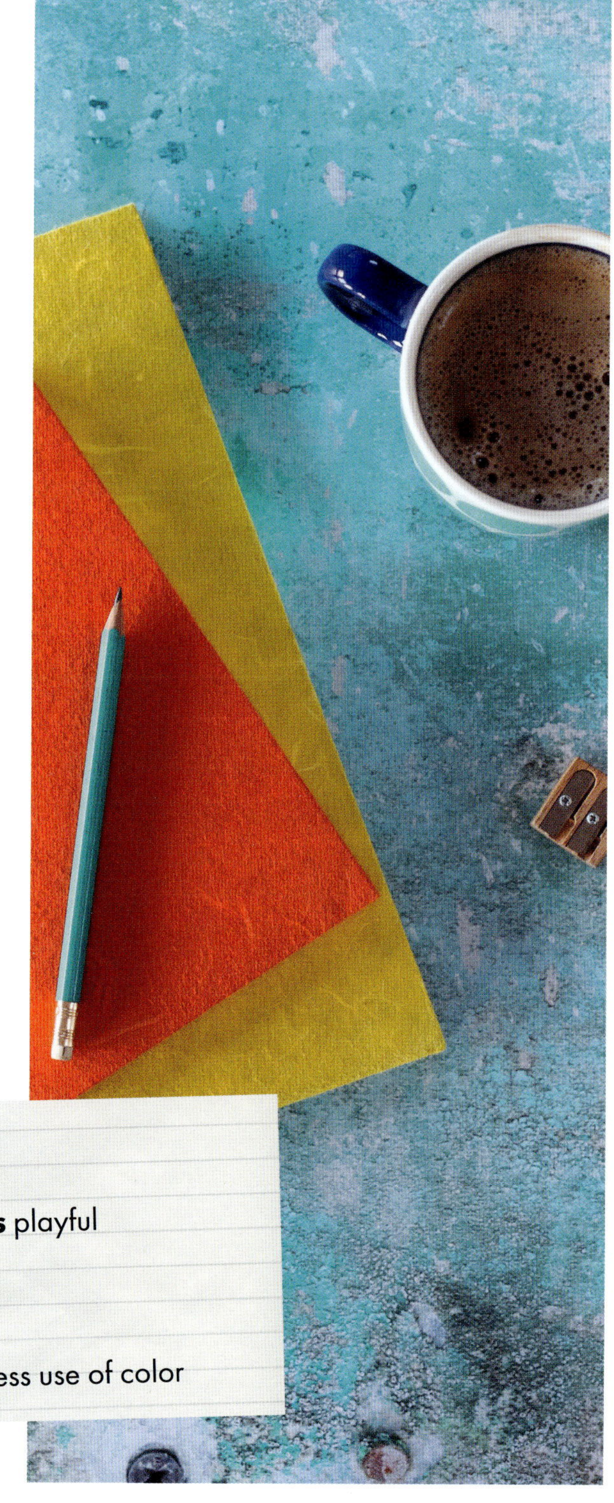

Fidgety **becomes** energetic

A silly sense of humor **becomes** playful

Emotional **becomes** layered

Spontaneous **becomes** a fearless use of color

Jot down your own personality traits and ask friends and family for help, as they may identify traits you hadn't considered. Once you've made that list, think of ways in which you can bring them within your creative work. For example, if you've identified "quiet," this might become "subtle" or "delicate".

I'm often told my work is instantly recognizable. In many of the classes I teach I regularly highlight the importance of developing a signature style, and the characteristics I've listed are the core ingredients of my work. Some pieces are all these things, whereas others may contain just two ingredients. Whichever combination I use, my personality is always present. Having confidence in my quirks has been a great way for me to attract clients and collaborations, and ultimately provide me with more authority in my teaching. So never underestimate the power of doing it your own way.

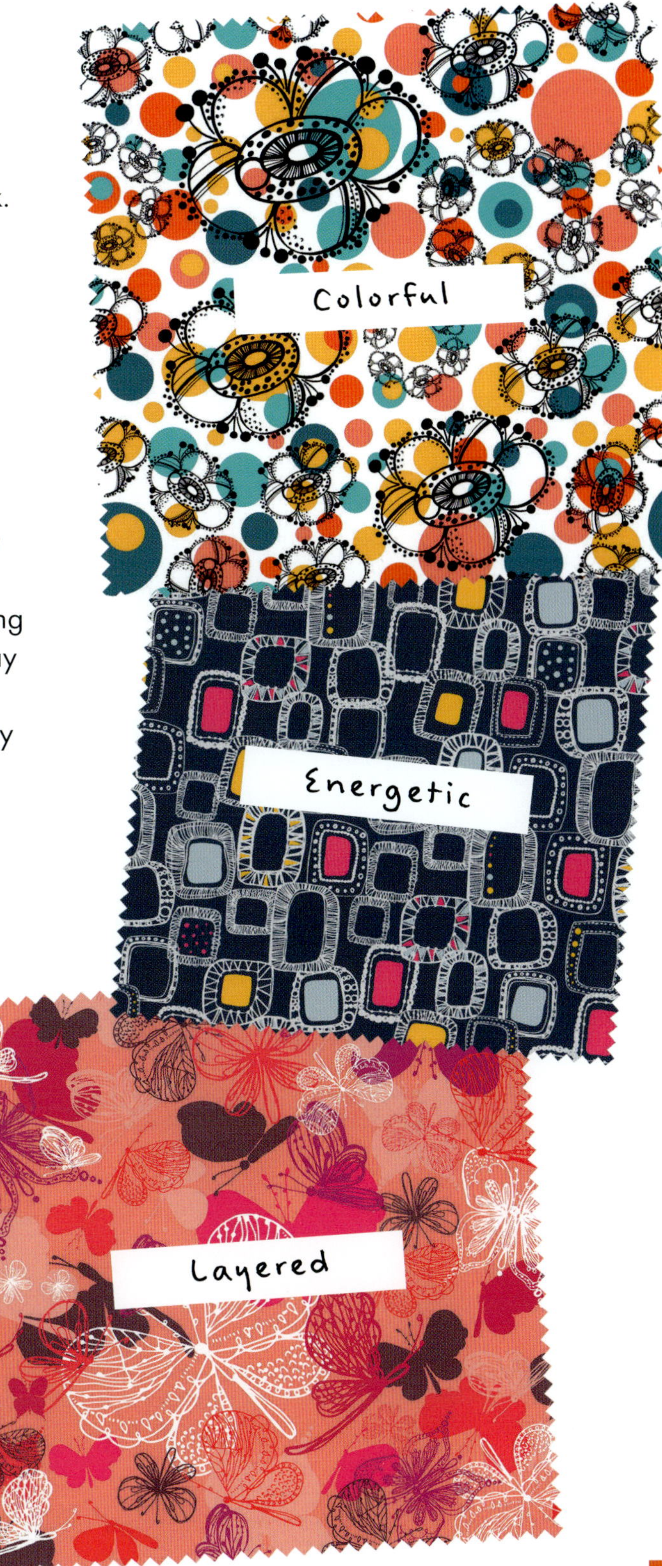

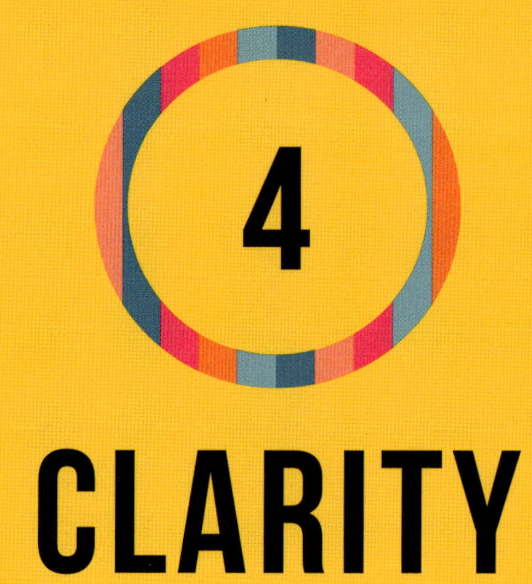

CLARITY

How do I clarify my vision?

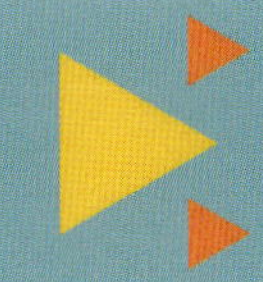

"Creation begins with vision."
—Henri Matisse

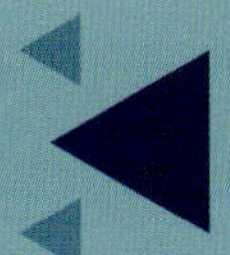

So many of us are often too afraid to clarify what is it is we really want. We change or shrink our ideas, dreams, and goals to feel more accepted. We say things like, "But it's not a big deal" or "Well, it might never happen." We want to avoid being perceived as an unrealistic dreamer, greedy, or even arrogant for daring to want to fulfill our desires.

Over the years I've begun to fully understand how important it is to clarify your own vision and say it out loud. If you don't know exactly what it is you want, how do you expect to turn that dream into a reality? We need to understand all the fundamentals of our vision to take action both consciously and subconsciously.

Clarifying your end goal is so important, and that can go hand in hand with clarifying who you are as a creative. If you've skipped ahead to this chapter, please revisit Chapter 1, BEGIN, and complete the dream conversation exercise—it's a great resource for helping to clarify your creative self.

You want to fall so in love with your idea, vision, or goal that it feels like a relationship you want to nourish. The more you are dedicated and passionate about it, the more energy and drive you will have to push through when things get tough. Take a moment to reflect during uncomfortable moments and remind yourself of the reason you are doing this and the love and bond you have built with your goal to ultimately make it happen.

But having said that, here's a gentle reminder that it's okay to change, evolve, or move on from what was once your dream. You are not obligated to be the same person you were yesterday or in the past; evolving is part of human nature and the creative process. Your ideas, goals, and dreams will naturally change along with you. This is something we will also talk about more in Chapter 8, LONGEVITY, and Chapter 9, DESTINATION.

After reading this chapter and working through these exercises, feel free to revisit it over time when perhaps you have come to a crossroads and need clarity in your creative life once again.

THOUGHTS TO PONDER ON CLARITY

Your vision could be so many things: your next piece of creativity, ideas for a project you've always wanted to complete, or a long-term life goal. Whatever it may be, sometimes zooming out to look at the bigger picture allows your mind to become clearer about your end goal and the purpose behind it. This will also aid with exploring your creative identity.

You may also want to consider that sometimes what you thought you wanted turns out to be very different in reality. It might not be what you expected or needed, and that's okay too, as you can simply reset. We all need to be able to give ourselves permission to have more than one finish line.

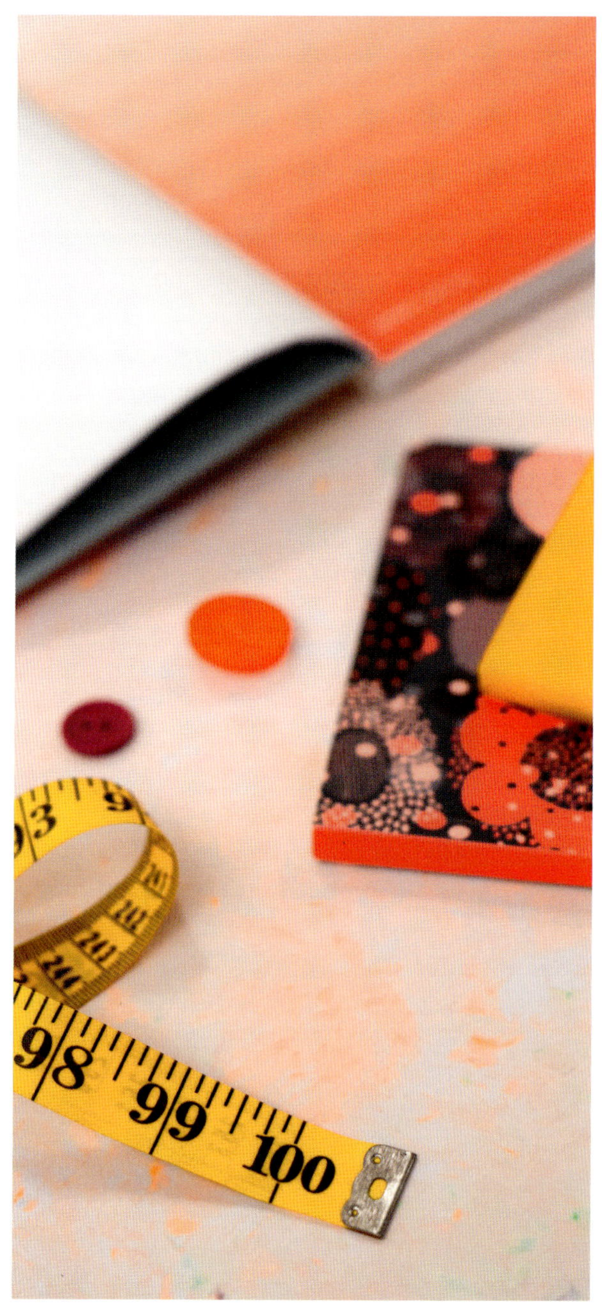

When things don't go how we expected, I love to say it's just a "plot twist" and carry on! Bumps in the road also help you appreciate the final result even more.

OWNING WHO YOU ARE CREATIVELY

If you struggle identifying what it is you want from your creativity, try listing what you *don't* want and why. It can be a real eye opener. My example is on the right.

Now try writing your own. I often find this exercise incredibly cleansing; you're saying goodbye to things you no longer want to accept in your life, and ultimately, you're making room for things you greatly welcome.

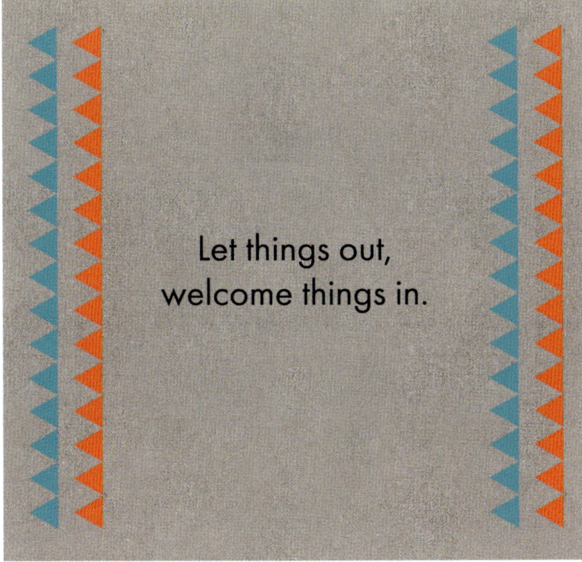

What I Don't Want to Work on Creatively

- Large artworks. I don't have the space for it.
- Projects that span across months. I get bored easily.
- Restricted color palettes. I get stressed if there's no variety in color.
- Intense and rigid hours. I need flexibility around family life.
- Regimented briefs. I much prefer if some areas can evolve more organically, because I work better and create more original art that way.

VISION BOARD

We can all dream dreams, but having something physically created is incredibly powerful. I don't stop at just one vision board; I usually recommend my clients create two, as it really helps you have a clear vision when it comes to manifesting what you really want. The reason I ask for two is so that my clients can become really clear on what they want from life both personally and professionally. Focus one on work and/or creative-orientated goals. What does it look like? Is it painting commissions, licensing deals, getting your photography published? For the second consider your ideal life. Does it include remote working? Part-time hours around family commitments? Working outdoors or abroad? If you can see it and believe it will happen, you will do everything you can to work toward it and achieve your goals.

I also think these are a great tool for dreaming big but also for setting realistic goals. For example, there's no point having a board that shows a six-month time frame and you want to create two or three children's books. Or if your personal vision board shows you yearn to work outdoors but your creative vision board involves a project that has you stuck inside. The more aligned we can be the better, as the happier we will be personally and the better results we will achieve creatively. At times the boards will naturally feed into each other, as many of us find so much joy from having creativity in our lives.

There will be moments when you have to put extra hours in or work flat out to get to achieve your professional goals, but please remember to also honor the dream from your personal vision board. Work/life balance is so important.

This exercise can be revisited time and time again. Naturally as life evolves your creativity and vision may change. I would also encourage you to keep all your vision boards. They are a great way of reflecting on what your goals once were, what you've achieved and where your dreams have taken you. It's a wonderful feeling when you reflect upon a vision board and know that you have achieved some or all of the things on it. Because at the time of making that board you probably would never have believed that you could do it. Each time you create a new board, why not dream that little bit bigger. There are no limits. Refer to chapter 9, DESTINATION about how changing your plans and goals is okay and might even be necessary sometimes.

Stay true to you and believe in your path.

SHARED EXPERIENCE

Here are a couple of great examples from one of my clients, Georgina Van Hasselt from the UK.

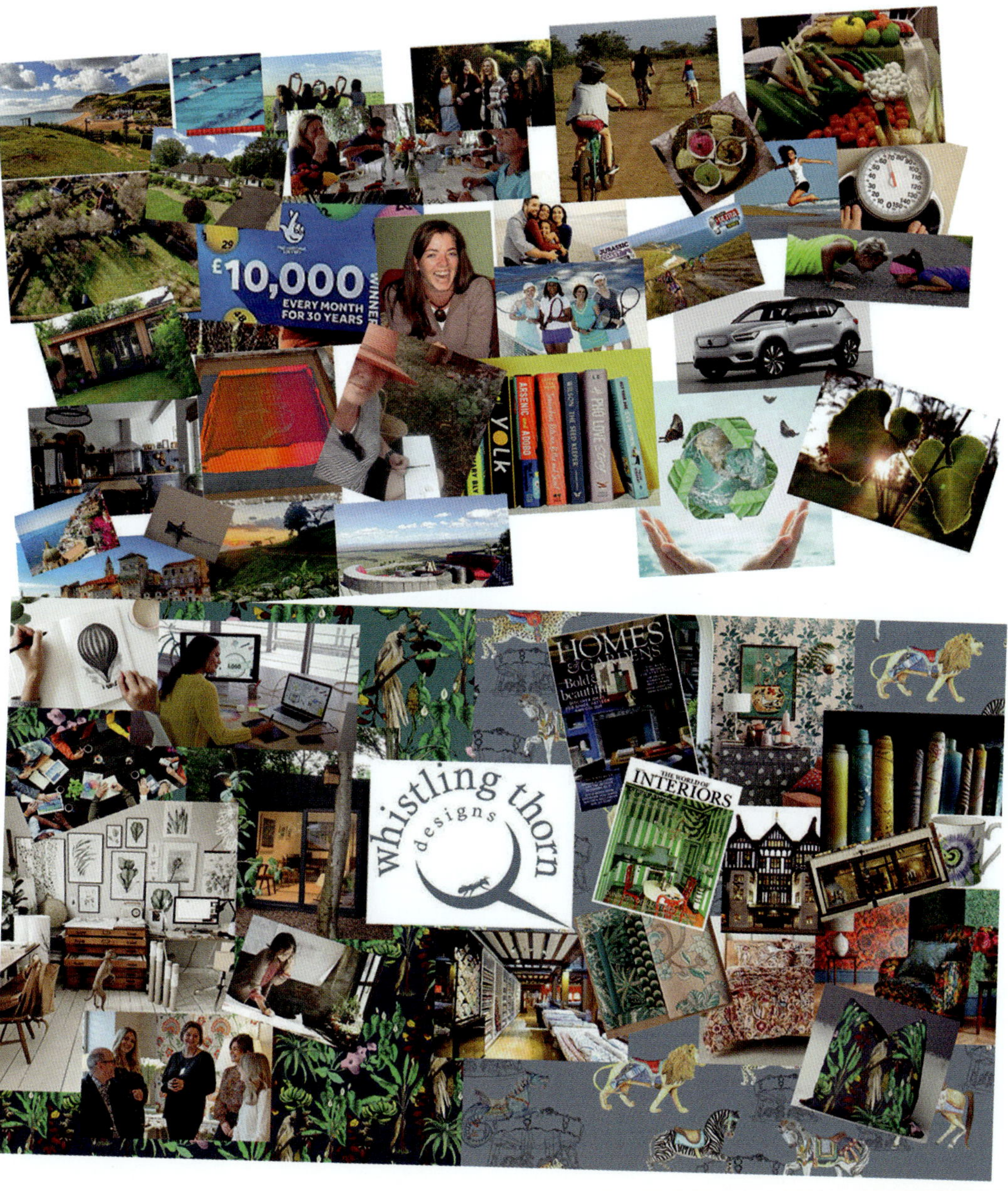

"For the work goals I focused on the working environment that I would like to create: the atmosphere, the space, and the feeling I wanted to create with the people I will work with once my company is at that stage. Rachael encouraged me to get clear on where I would like to see my business in the future. I would like to see my wallpaper, fabrics, and home accessories in stores such as Liberty and Anthropologie.

My personal board covered different aspects of family life that I wanted to work toward or had envisaged. It was a great reminder of the things that bring me joy, some of which had fallen by the wayside.

As a creative, visual imagery has more of an impact than words, and this exercise helps me keep focus and drive things forward. It really is a great reminder, especially when you have it as a screen saver or up on a wall where you can see it."

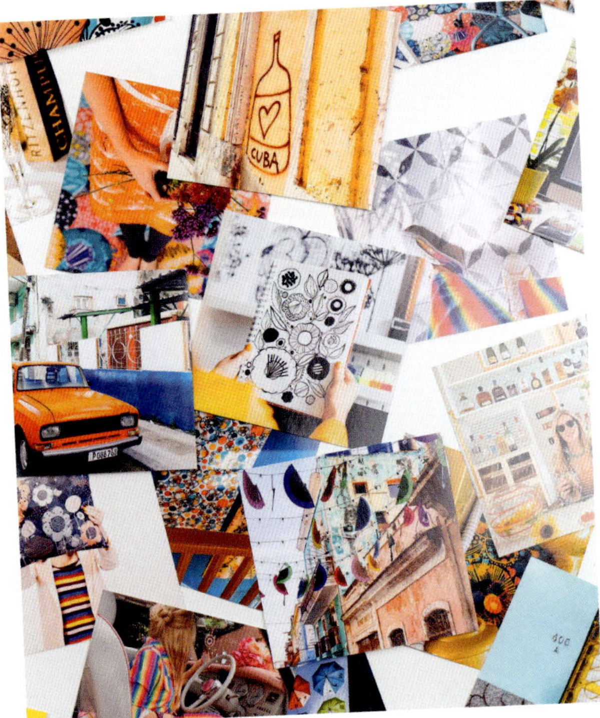

You can create these boards digitally and keep them on the computer or print them out. Or you can make them physically by cutting and sticking lots of images or inspirational key words you may have collected. Cherish these for life.

I like to see them as a scrapbook of what my future will look like. It's great when later down the line you realize your life looks exactly (or similar) to what you visually manifested. It really does work, but you have to put the hard work, passion, and dedication in too!

DON'T FIXATE ON THE WHAT IF, FIXATE ON WHAT CAN I DO?

Even when we feel we know who we are creatively, when thinking of a new idea or identifying what we really want, we can hit an obstacle before we have even started. Worrying about failure, taking risks, and thinking about all of the unknown factors can steer our minds into overdrive and stifle our creativity. To combat this, learn to recognize what your strengths are and what you can make happen now. Take it one step at a time and remember that small steps can really make big things happen.

I drafted my own list of strengths recently and I often look at it when I'm feeling lost or overwhelmed. It can be a great thing to pin on your wall alongside your vision boards:

- I'm unstoppable with my creativity.
- I'm fearless with color.
- My designs make people feel energized and happy.
- I bring a sense of fun with everything I create.
- My creations are contemporary with a retro twist.
- I celebrate my passions and heritage through my creative output.
- I'm intuitive and organic and often design ahead of the trends.
- I can manage my time, the time of others and balance multiple projects with ease—well, most of the time!
- I'm perfectly imperfect.
- I uplift, motivate, and inspire.
- My designs and words can make others feel amazing.
- I help people achieve their dreams.

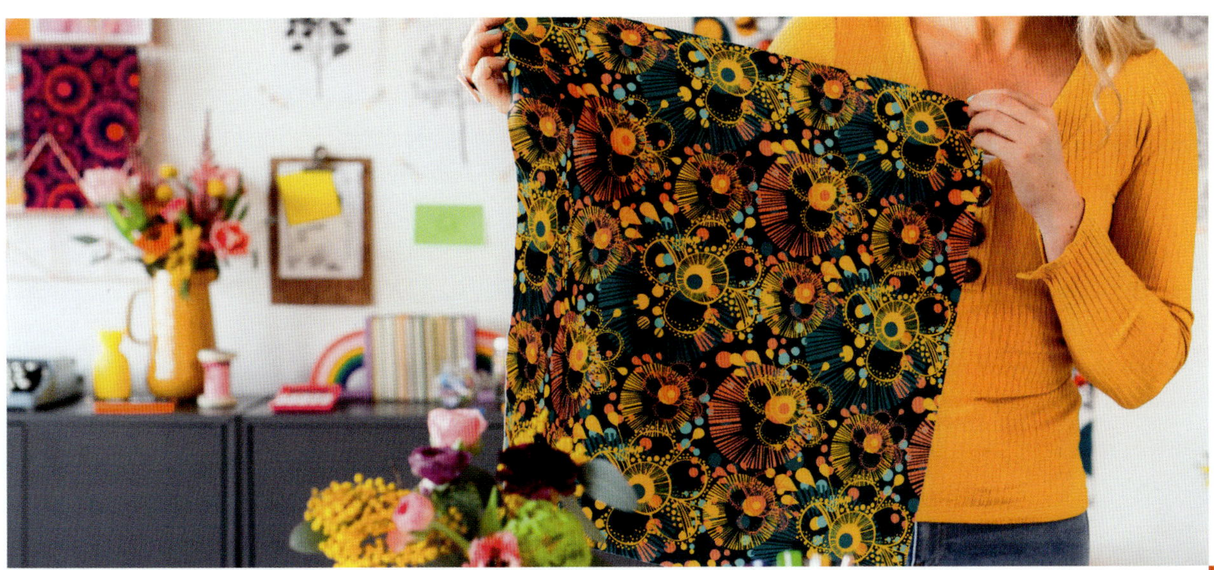

SAYING IT OUT LOUD

Often at the start of most of my coaching sessions, the first thing I ask is: "Tell me your dream—not the smaller dream you often share with others. What's the big dream? If anything were possible. Close your eyes and don't hold back."

That initial big dream is so important. We often think that big dreams are so out of reach, but a dream is just an idea that needs a plan of action. When I highlight the small but powerful steps they can take to get there, that dream no longer seems impossible.

I urge you to aim for the top and be unapologetic about what you want in life. ***Say it out loud.*** Life is short, precious, magical, and amazing, but can be tough sometimes. Don't deny what your creative heart wants. You might have to chip away at it, or put it on hold at times, but you owe it to yourself to give it the best chance you can.

Stating my intention that I wanted to teach and travel more on social media really helped. Before I knew it, I was contacted with more teaching opportunities, and I made progress with my creative projects out in Cuba. I also welcomed trying to learn Spanish that year, and as I absorbed more cultural influences my creative work was all the better for it.

Another year my keyword was *freedom*. I'm a better person when I feel free. While I always strive for this, I'm a realist too. I know there will always be mundane things I need to do and responsibilities that pull me away, but I try to focus on having freedom in my life as much as I realistically can.

Success is for everyone
(not just the people
you admire).

So while I have goals—where I ***will*** write a series of books and collaborate with a dream fashion brand—I make sure to weave them into my life in ways that allow me to embrace freedom. The underlying factor is always that I'm a single mum and crave quality time with my son. Having freedom around this keeps me happy, which then ultimately fuels my creativity for the better.

Note that I didn't say *hopefully* and that I wrote *I will* as if it will happen. Our mind-set and the language we use is just as important as outlining the vision. You must see it and *believe* in it! Positive language is important, especially when talking about ourselves or what we're working on. There's more to explore on mind-set and language in Chapter 6, MOTIVATION.

SHARED EXPERIENCE

One of my coaching clients, Lindsay Elissa Coils from the UK, struggled with identifying her dream, and her instant reaction was to answer *"to pay the bills."* And yes, we all need to pay our bills, but this was her shrinking her dreams rather than embracing bigger opportunities for herself, opportunities that could allow her to pay her bills and then some—potentially giving her more flexibility and financial freedom.

After we chatted, I encouraged Lindsay to speak her creative truth, and she outlined all the products she wanted to design as well as her client wish list. Then we broke it down into simple steps and a plan. Saying this out loud brought her so much clarity, and I reminded her that if she put the work in, she's as deserving of success as much as anyone.

"I feel like I can put together an action plan from our chat and push myself forward. I'm hoping that by setting myself mini goals in the months ahead I can be in a completely different mind-set by Christmas and hopefully have bagged myself at least one new client. Not hopefully, I will. See? It's working already . . ."

ACTION PLAN EXAMPLES

DREAM 1: *Create X designs for X products.*

1. Market research—scope out the competition.
2. Product research—how much does it cost to make X.
3. Manufacturing/printing research—where can I get X made.
4. Test out X designs on X product mock-ups.
5. Get X designs printed on X products.
6. Photograph X products.
7. Put X products on my website and/or social media.

DREAM 2: *Get my work sold to/in X.*

1. Research X and the designs they like to sell/buy.
2. Design a pdf to pitch to X with a cover letter and relevant imagery.
3. Make sure website and/or social media is up-to-date.
4. Send email and/or pitch pdf to X.
5. Follow up with X; if I don't hear, move on to the next opportunity!

CONSTRUCTIVE CRITICISM

When working on something new, we often seek advice, support, and reassurance. Think about who you *actually* want to speak to for supportive, constructive criticism.

It happens often that when I've spoken to family and friends, some have been really supportive, whereas others sometimes don't know how to provide the support I need and don't understand my entrepreneurial spirit. It doesn't mean they don't love me and don't want me to do well, it's just that we're from different backgrounds. But it's important to have people around you who are going to give you valid feedback from experience.

An example would be this time when a good friend had said to me that they didn't think anyone would buy an online course. If I had listened to them, then I wouldn't be where I am today, and Make It In Design wouldn't exist. So as good as it can be to get feedback, you want to get the right type of constructive feedback and not let any naysayers or people who just don't get your vision put you off. Trust your instincts. If you've worked hard and you've been dedicated, your idea is going to go out there into the world and do really well for you because you've put the work in and you've shown up.

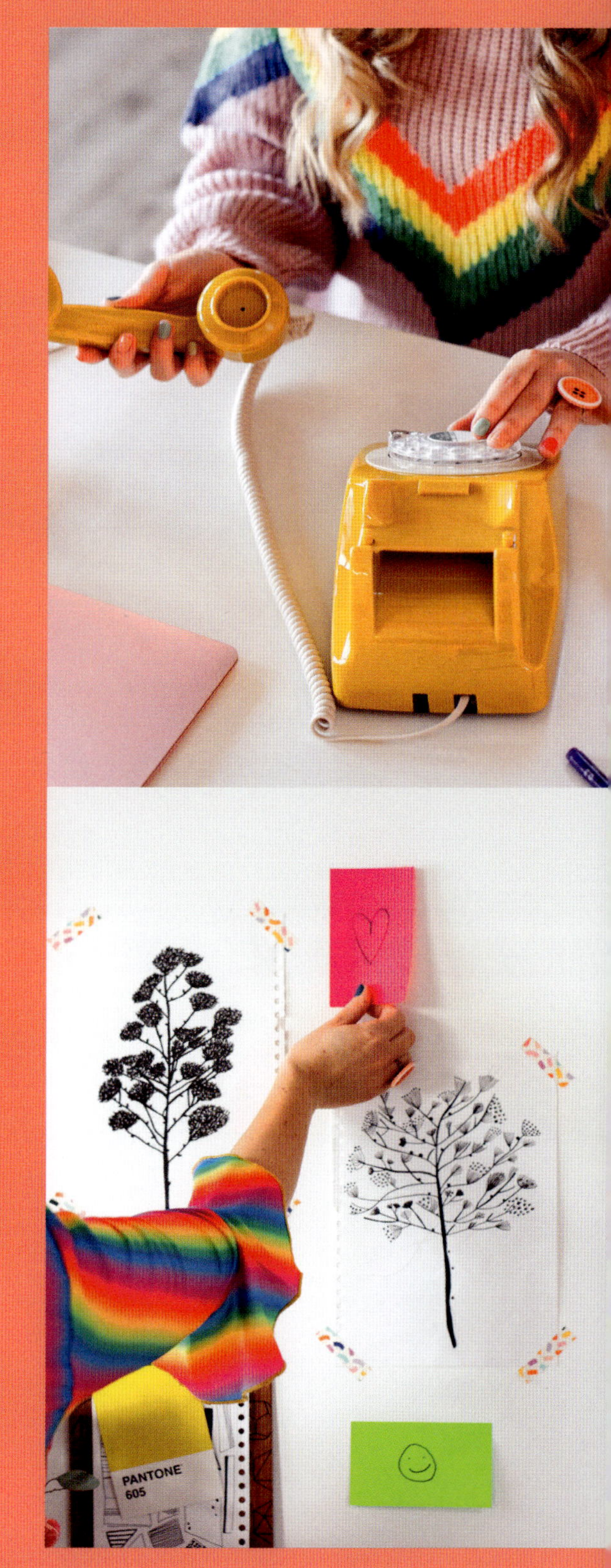

To support this, try drafting a list of around five to eight people whom you can regularly go to for advice and inspiration (sometimes you may need to broaden this list). It can be reassuring to form a bubble with others because sometimes we just need others to see our work. As creative people, we can obsess over perfecting things so much that our ideas never make it out into the real world. Here's who I often go to for feedback, support, and constructive criticism:

- My business partner and fellow Make It In Design cofounder Beth Kempton. She has a wonderful way with words, is business savvy and analytical, and has great entrepreneurial spirit.

- My studio manager Kelly Crossley. She's an all-round talented creative who understands what I'm trying to say even when sometimes I can't quite articulate it myself.

- Design peers. There are a few go-getter design peers I often send previews of or final links for projects to and they can offer an experienced yet fresh perspective.

- My global design community. I'll often float ideas out there to my students and alumni. Some know me well and some may have only just signed up for a class. I know that they will be very honest and tell me what they need, want, liked, and disliked.

- Last but not least, my mum. She is forever the person to show me what real strength is. She tells me to follow my heart, encourages me to follow my dreams, and reminds me to work hard but more importantly to stop for air and have some fun.

If I hadn't had feedback from these people, then this book, something I had worked on for so long, might not have happened. I wrote bits here and there, left scrappy notes, and had a mind whirling with perfectly imperfect ideas, but often I was too scared to show anyone. Once I let people in, they could offer advice and constructive feedback and help me discover some real light bulb moments that in turn made this book the best it could be.

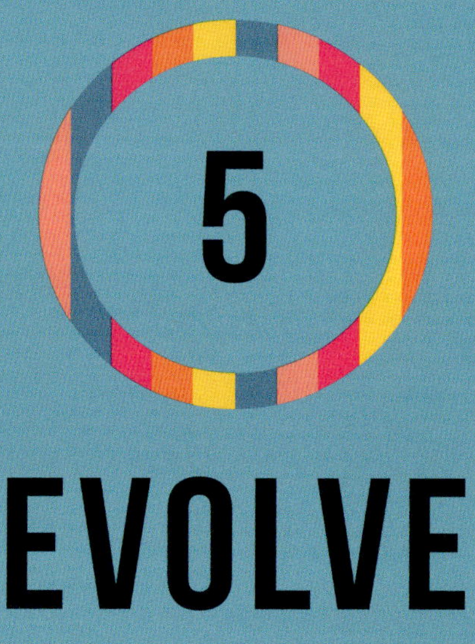

EVOLVE

Do I need to evolve?

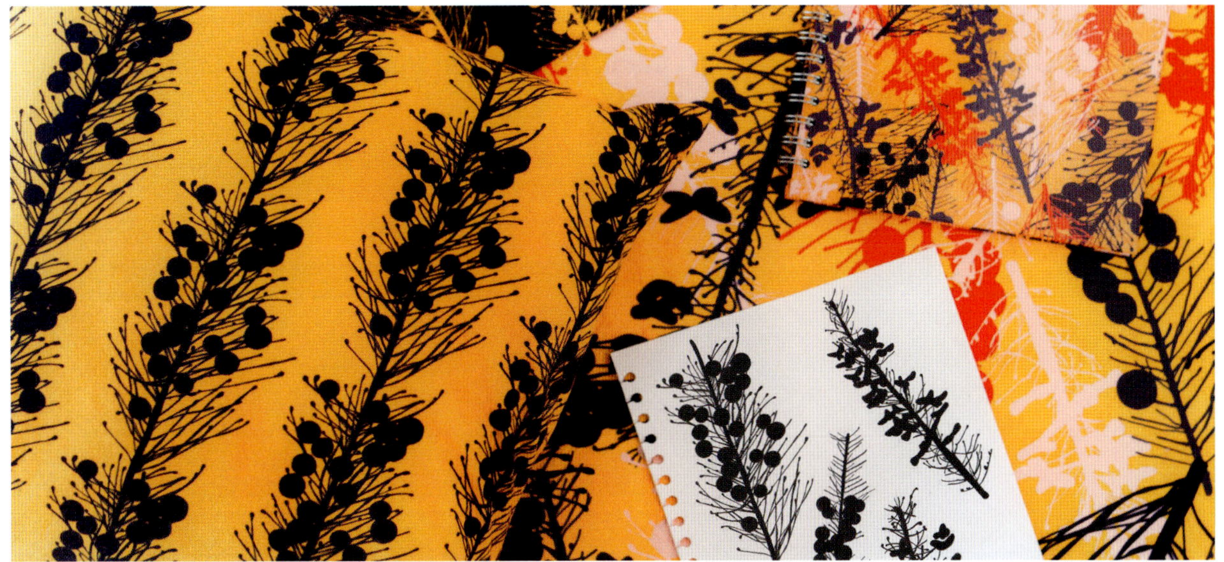

So many of us fantasize about a way of life, a dream commission or collaboration, or just trying something new, but we don't do anything to put the wheels in motion or adapt to make room for growth or change. It's so easy to be comfortable and at times complacent, and while we might be ticking along nicely, before we know it, we can be become stagnant in our creativity.

One example of this is when I became so stuck in a rut with my creative work. Floral and nature-based art is my strength, and what I was most known for in the early stages of my career. But after I'd been doing the same thing over and over for many years, and even though I was having success with it, I became so withdrawn when making art and I felt I'd lost my inspiration.

I took a break, and even if it was subconsciously done at the time, I began to evolve my process. By switching it up and doing simple things, such as documenting florals through the seasons, from full bloom to dying seed heads, I was able to create much more unique motifs. I found this technique really useful, particularly when it comes to drawing popular flowers such as alliums and lilies. As creatives we're often given a much-loved subject matter that's been represented thousands of times before, and we can feel overwhelmed when we want to put our own stamp on things. Flipping our perspective can work wonders.

Another example would be when I took a hit financially in business, I remember feeling so shocked by it. Once I got through the initial upset and let my bruised ego heal, I realized that a big kick up the bum was what I really needed to analyze my projects. I don't think business and life has been the same since, and I now embrace change with even more open arms.

THOUGHTS TO PONDER ON EVOLVING

It's important to recognize that growth can be uncomfortable and painful but also necessary and beautiful. I always think of the cocoon period for a butterfly and the end result becoming something truly wonderful.

Change can be difficult at first, for us and sometimes for those around us. We all become comfortable with familiarity and question our need to rock the boat or try something different. Often there is a struggle or learning period before we can reap the rewards of change. While not everyone will understand your need to evolve and some may even mock you for it, I urge you to not make decisions solely based on the influence of others. It's *your* creative life, so never live it for someone else. Trust your instincts and do your best to explain what's necessary to those around you, but ultimately you owe it to yourself to make the change you want to make.

While talking about growth, I also want to highlight the importance of not putting so much pressure on yourself. At the time of writing this, a new year had just begun and with it the stress that can often come with not having completed the to-do list from last year or failing to achieve what I wanted. For some people, the whole "new year, new you" thing can be a great motivation, but for others it can just feel like unnecessary pressure. Growth is a process, and it needs to happen when it's right for you. Never feel the "old you" is bad or inadequate when the rest of the world makes huge declarations about their past achievements or future aspirations.

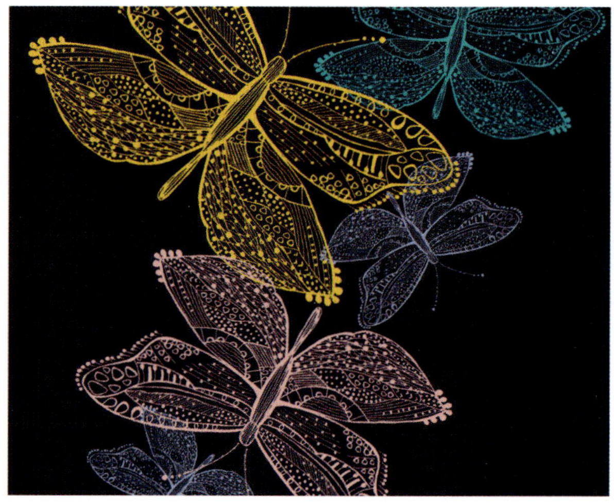

I also think we don't give ourselves enough credit when it comes to change. Sometimes we are so caught up in the doing that we can forget to reflect on what we've achieved, how we learned a new skill or tried something different that made us evolve for the better.

In life we experience both the good and the bad; without realizing it, the tough situations can make us change for the better and help us become stronger and more resilient to navigate life.

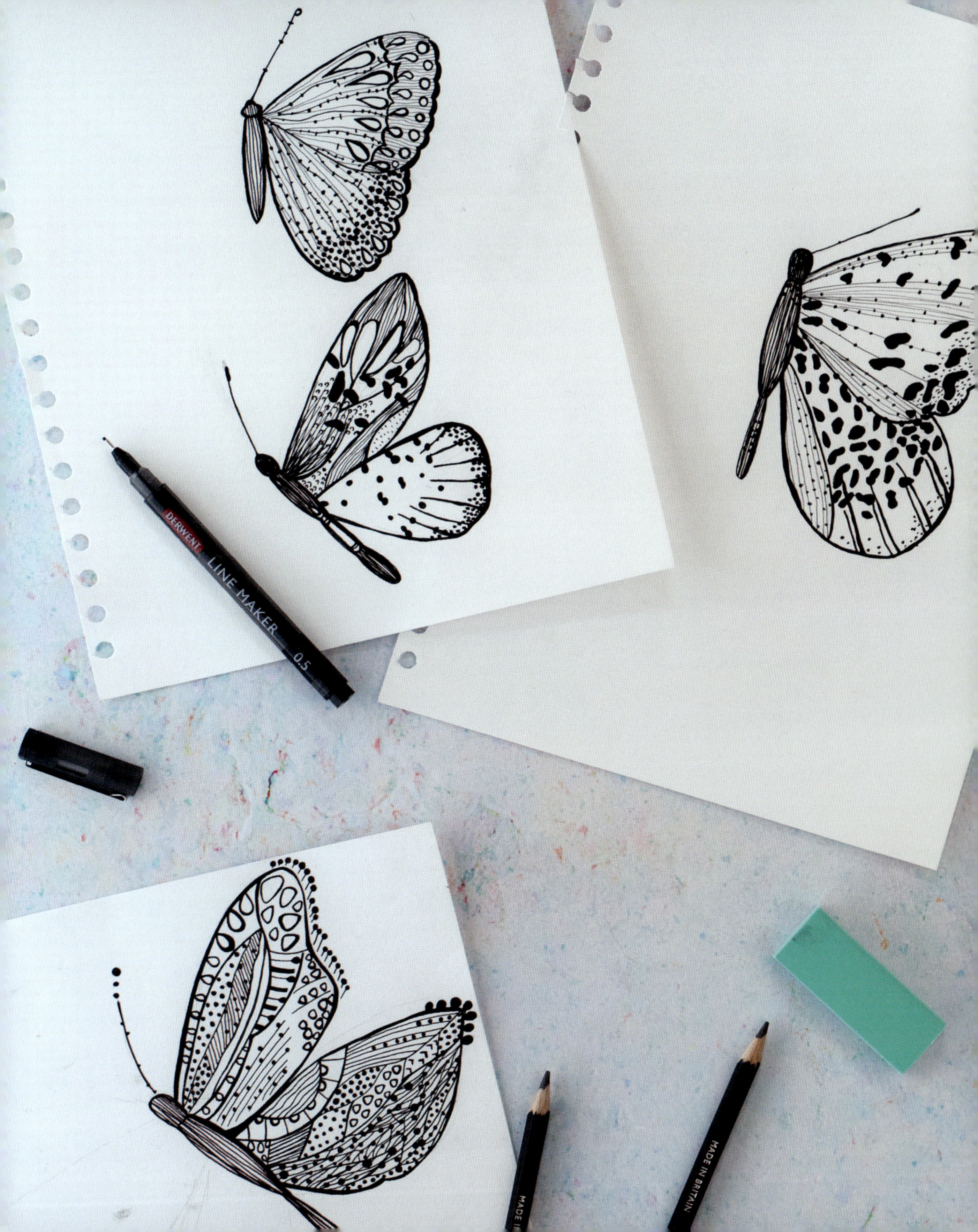
DERWENT
LINE MAKER
0.5
MADE IN BRITAIN

CREATIVE EXERCISES

PERSONAL AND PROFESSIONAL DEVELOPMENT

There are many simple practices that spur us on for growth and personal development, some we might favor more than others. For me, having conversations, listening to others, and exploring this big wide and amazing world we live in help me be a better person both personally and professionally. Here are the things that help my development. What are yours?

- Travel
- Books
- Workshops
- Online classes
- Conversation
- Listening

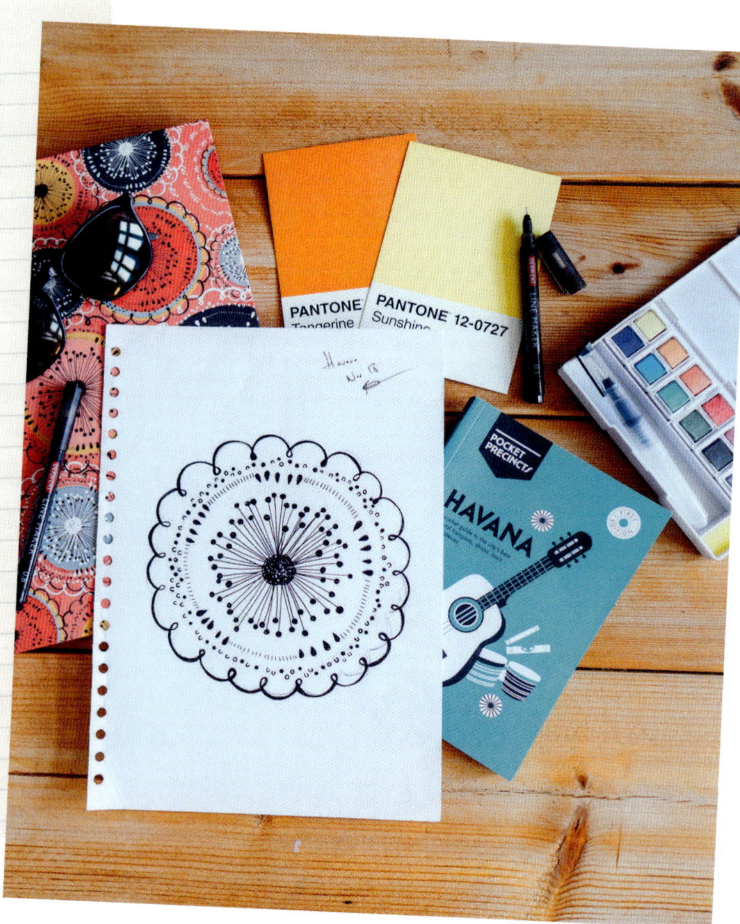

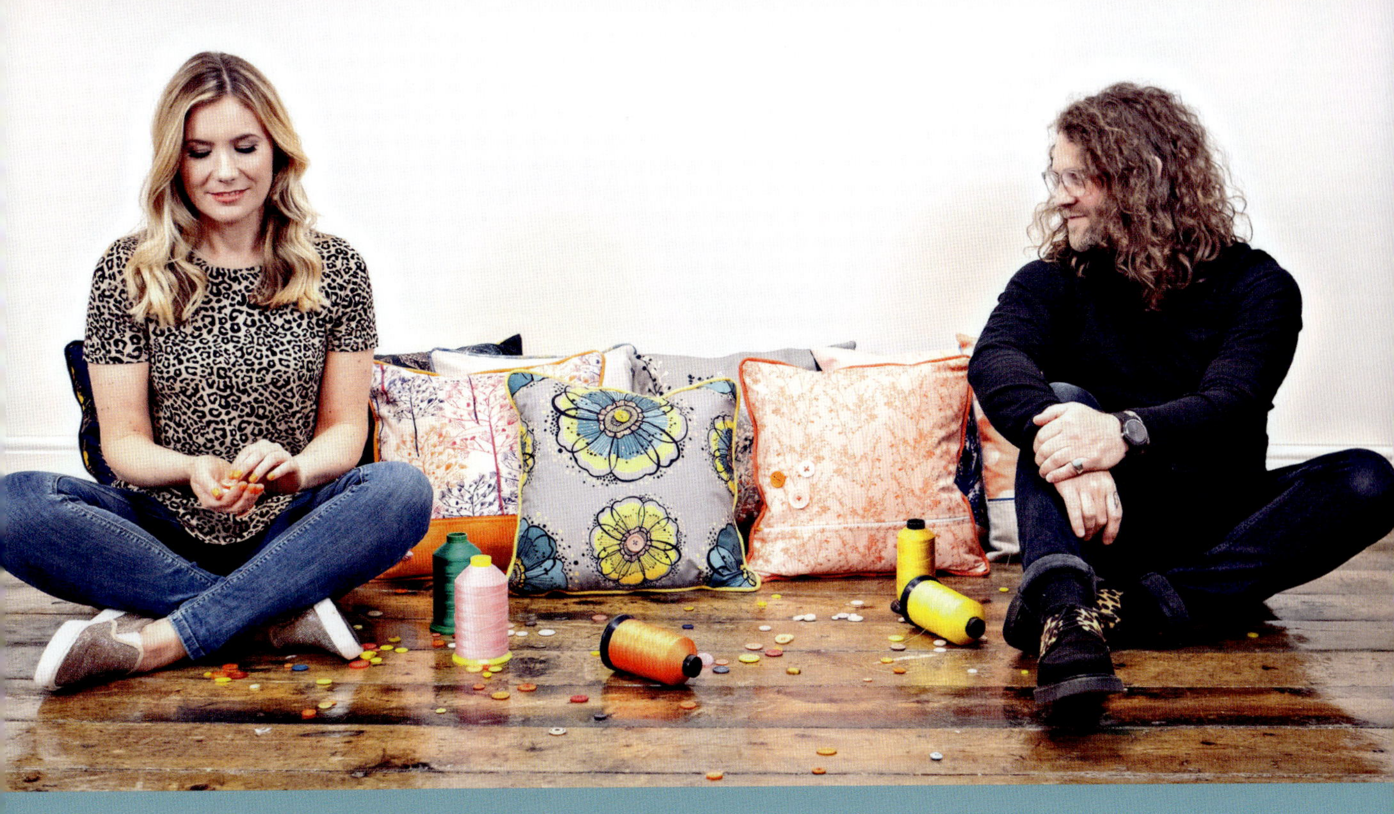

THE POWER OF COLLABORATION

Many creatives can work solo and shy away from interaction, myself included, but I have found it can become very detrimental to my health and creative energy. Some of my best creations and projects have happened as a result of conversations, learning from others, or joining forces and collaborating. In fact, Make It In Design and this book would never have been born without working with others.

The creative community can get so much from one another, from encouragement and support to a second opinion when moments of self-doubt creep in. New ideas can be born, skills learned or improved, jobs shared and found, and competitions entered. What I've found through Make It In Design is that the creative community is truly worldwide, and if we open our eyes to different experiences and cultural offerings, then there is no limit to our creative possibilities.

I feel so inspired by other creatives, and I love to go to events to network. I've heard many stories of my students forming collaborative groups and collectives and exhibiting their work together around the world. I think this is such an amazing idea. So my challenge for you is to reach out to others to see what opportunities there can be!

FEAR OF CHANGE

Take a moment to think about what might be stopping you from making a change. Has there been a period in your life where you needed to make a change but perhaps you shied away from it out of fear, and maybe that led you to miss a creative opportunity? As you take a trip down memory lane, consider the change you want to make, what it is you're afraid of or what is stopping you, and what you can do to remove the obstacle or fear. Jot down some notes on a pad or in your journal. You can see some of my own examples below.

The change I want to make	What's stopping me or what am I afraid of?	What can I do to remove that obstacle or fear?
Try new design themes and motifs in my work.	Losing my client base because they like what I do already.	Just give it a go as I already have lots of work archived that clients will like and I'm likely to attract new clients.
Use a new technique or software.	Being bad at it and not getting good results.	Believing in my abilities and training and knowing that experimentation is just part of the creative process.
Expanding my creative writing portfolio.	People judging me: "She's a designer, not a writer".	Remind myself that my audience has appreciated my authentic (and imperfect) writing so far, through my courses and magazine articles. The more I write, the more confidence I'll gain.

SHARED EXPERIENCE

Monica Escobar, an artist from Colombia, reached out to me at a moment when her creative work was taking off and she needed to decide between keeping her easy, comfortable job and making more time to invest in her creative passions. Here is what she answered:

The change I want to make	What's stopping me or what am I afraid of?	What can I do to remove that obstacle or fear?
Making more time for my passions and wanting things enough to believe they can be true.	I'm afraid of rejection and failure.	The more I do it, the easier it will get.

Monica has since dedicated two more days a week to her creative job, set herself a realistic target, and is working harder than ever to make it full time.

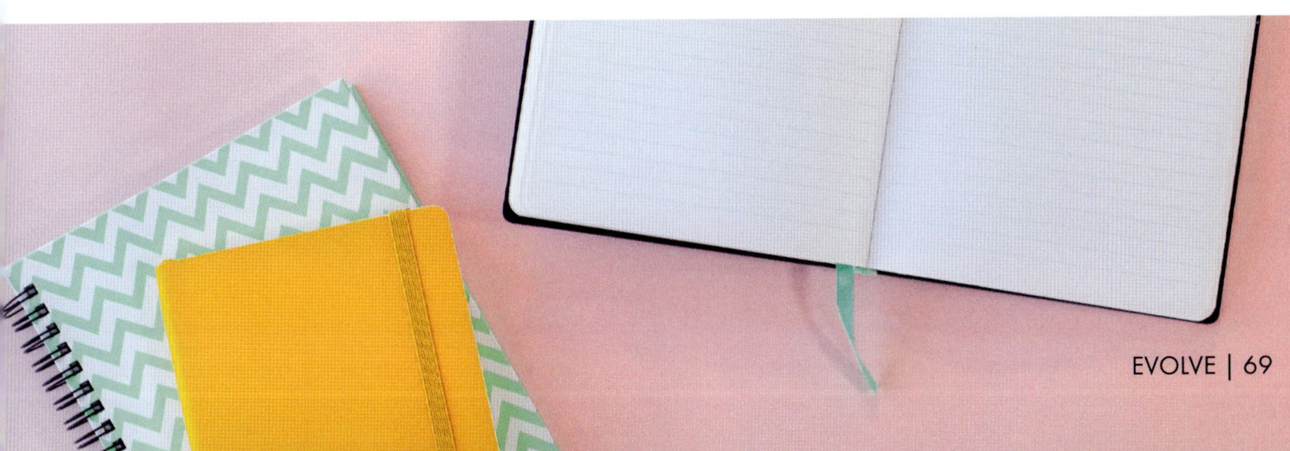

BEING A CREATIVE NOMAD

Over time we might be asked to evolve or quickly adapt to a new situation or environment and that has been the case for many since the Covid-19 pandemic.

The term "digital nomad" has become widely popular, with many living their lives and creating work on their own terms across a multitude of locations, or sometimes thrown into the deep end adapting as their work situation suddenly changed. For a digital nomad, it can mean sitting with a simple notepad or laptop in a remote environment. A "creative nomad," however, may need a wider array of tools in their kit, from paints to sketchbooks and even a lightweight easel. My own personal kit is simply a couple of sketchbooks, preferably in different sizes, and a pencil case with several drawing pens. I typically carry about twenty pens at any given time, as I favor drawing with different weights. I also carry a camera, though mostly these days I rely on my trusty iPhone and my small MacBook.

Occasionally you may find me taking an online meeting or pinging fast instant messages to my team. On a Cuban work trip, I experienced challenging Wi-Fi access, but still I found a way to muddle through, as I would download the bits I needed rather than staying connected. You can work from anywhere these days if you have the determination and drive to make it happen and actually do the work without getting too distracted.

The nomadic style of working and/or creating is far easier if you're self-employed or if you're typically in a work-from-home or freelance situation, as flexibility is one of the key factors to making it work. If your situation differs, however, please don't worry, it doesn't mean it's impossible! Like with anything in life if we want something there's always a way of making it work. You may be fitting in your creativity in your spare time or trying to work around a busy family life. Whatever your situation, I encourage you to also explore this nomadic approach. Change can be daunting at first, yet can also be an incredibly refreshing and rewarding experience, and I truly believe we can all reap the rewards by embracing the example of a nomadic lifestyle, even through small changes.

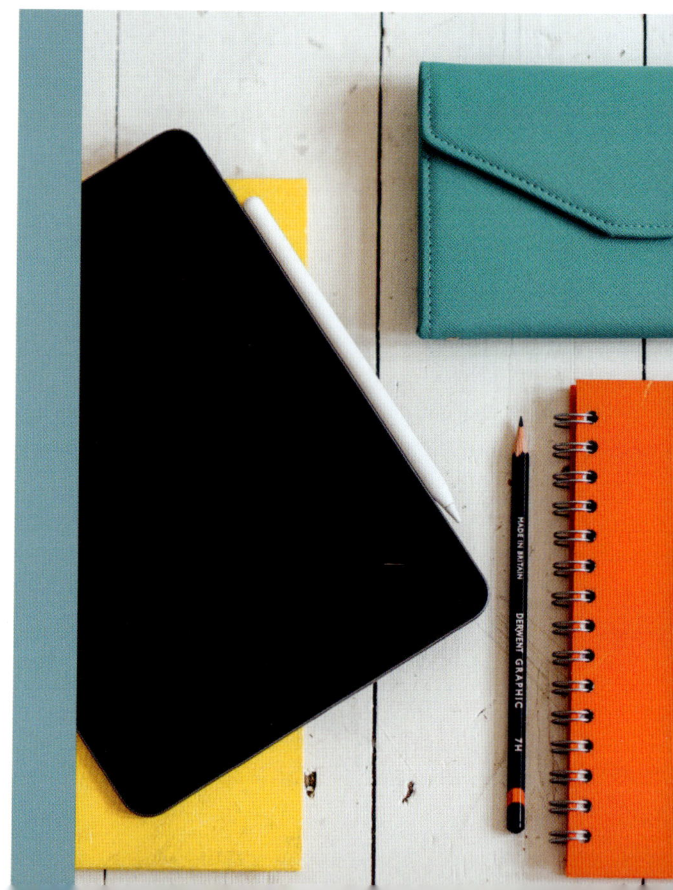

- **Visit two new locations this week,** even if it's just for a couple of hours: Set up a table in a relative's or friend's garden. Pack a lunch or picnic and visit a local park, garden, or beach. If you're restricted, then sitting by a window or on a balcony is a good alternative. It's all about the fresh air!

- **Set timed goals** and whizz through the admin and to-do lists.

- **Purposely leave all digital distractions at home** and enjoy drawing time and creative freedom.

- **Keep a journal.** Every time you break away from your usual environment, keep a note in your diary of time spent and tasks completed, and also write down your general thoughts and feelings about each experience. Use all of these to measure your productivity and analyze where you work at your best.

- **Make the most of your time.** Jot down all the inspiration that you see around you. Are there floor tiles? Are there patterned cushions, mosaics, tree shadows, geometric details? What's the mood or atmosphere like? Allow your subconscious to absorb the surroundings so you'll be fresh with creative ideas for the future.

I can't always work nomadically due to life and family commitments, and it also depends on what specific project I'm working on at the time. However, by naturally absorbing the nomadic mind-set, I mix up my routine at least once a week, and I can always see the positive impact that it has. If you're someone who works alone a lot, getting out and about and having an ever-changing workspace can really boost your mood and confidence levels and help you evolve your creative practice.

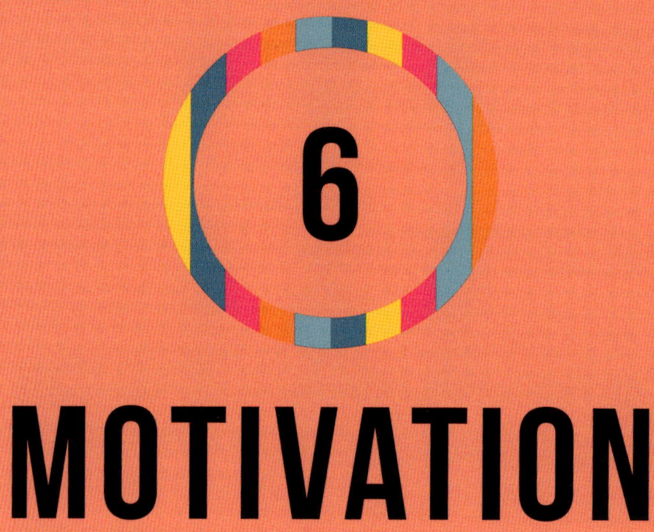

6 MOTIVATION

How do I stay motivated?

Over the years I've witnessed so many talented creatives produce the most beautiful work who then shy away and hide it, don't have the motivation to do anything with it, or don't know how to take the next step with their projects. I've found that even some of the most naturally gifted artists can feel lost or find themselves at a creative stumbling block. It can affect them so much that they don't know where to begin, so perhaps they don't begin at all.

We can power up our creativity in many ways, but without motivation how do we create? How do we find the drive to wake up each day and complete that next step, which is going to get us closer to achieving our creative dreams? When we feel energized to act, we can focus on the good things in our lives and find our motivation. Here are some ways you can stay motivated:

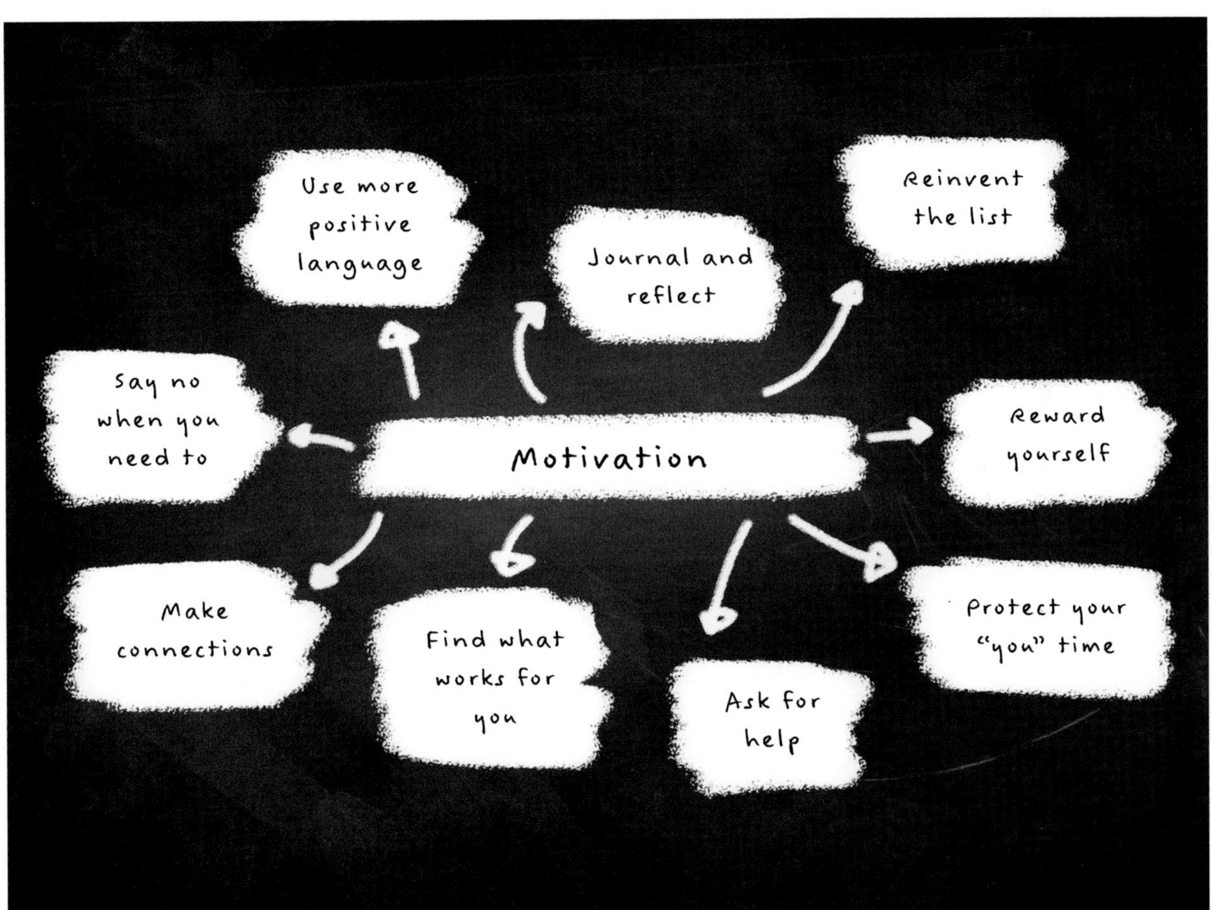

THOUGHTS TO PONDER ON MOTIVATION

Start your day with
"I get to"
rather than "I have to."

When you're working hard on something, or you're picking up your kids from school, or you're juggling another job, or going to the gym, or looking after someone, you can get caught up in the thought pattern of "I have to . . ." But what happens if you change the language and the mind-set that goes with that and say, "I get to . . ."? How does it change how you feel when you use more positive language?

On those days when I'm feeling like everything's just getting on top of me, I try to take a step back and think, "I get to work on this," "I get to do this project," "I get to pick up my son from school," "I get to cook this meal," or "I get to go food shopping." I think we all need the reminder sometimes that these are things that we take for granted.

So for today I'd like you to rewrite your to-do list another way. Instead of your life being "busy" today, try thinking "life is full." It's amazing that we even have things to do and being grateful for them can work wonders.

You might be doing a task daily that's someone else's dream and it's so easy to become complacent. Here is my example for today:

*Today I **get** to wake up warm and comfy, eat a nice breakfast, hug my son and take him to school, walk the dog, tidy up, reply to (a lot) of emails, drive my cute pink car, go to a lunchtime yoga class, write for my deadline, plan a photoshoot, attempt some admin, pick up my son from after school club, cook dinner, write to friends, call my mum, and catch up on my creativity, life, and DIY in general.*

I totally take all these amazing small things for granted (especially when I'm tired), but now I'll have a fresh perspective!

The topic of positive language is an important one throughout this book because I know it can make such a big impact on how we see, feel, and output our creativity. Often when we say things like, "I need to do this," or "I need to get this finished," it can add to the weight on our shoulders, and we can feel more stressed or pressured. However, if we switch that up and rephrase it more like "I'm going to do this," or "I'm going to finish this," then automatically we start to feel a little bit better. Changing the language that you use is like giving yourself a pep talk, so that rather than feeling like you *need* to do something you *want* to do it.

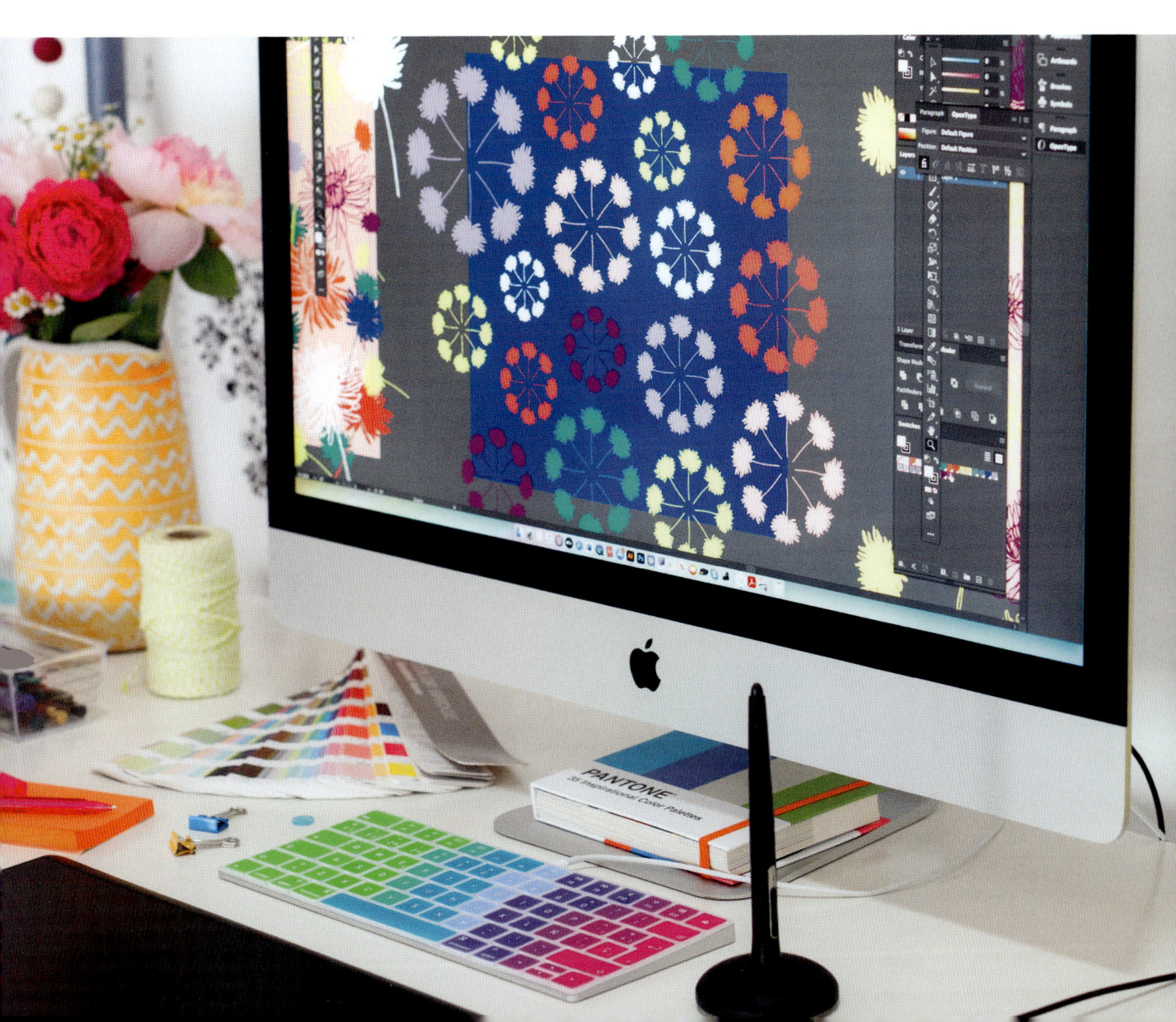

JOURNALING

A simple way of recognizing bad habits, and the things that keep us unmotivated, is to journal those thoughts and doubts and go-to words that you use daily. At the end of the week, reflect upon the way in which you talk to yourself. If it seems like you are only using negative language, then you know something has to change. You would root for your best friend to succeed, you'd motivate, encourage, support, and inspire them, so why do you treat yourself any differently?

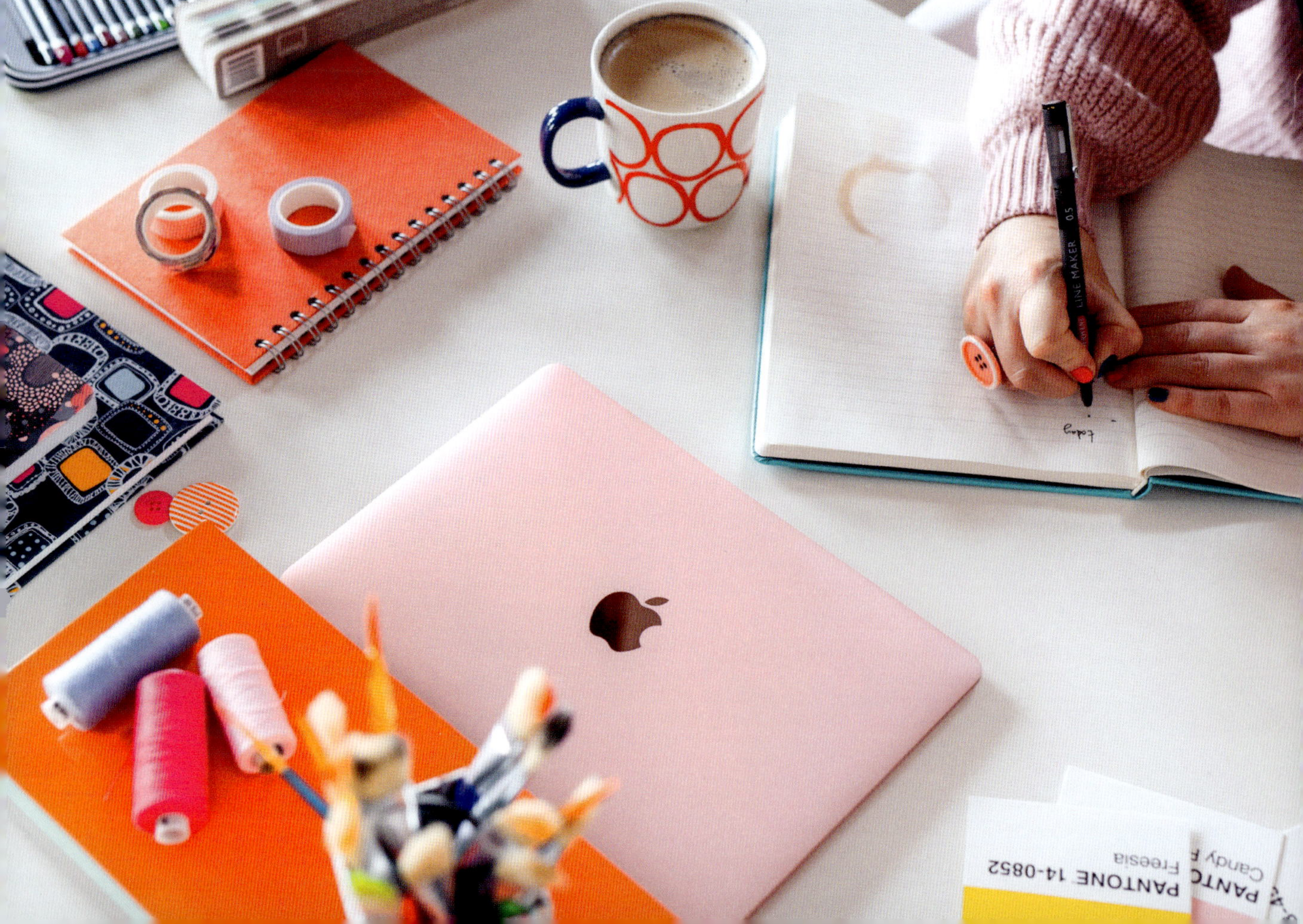

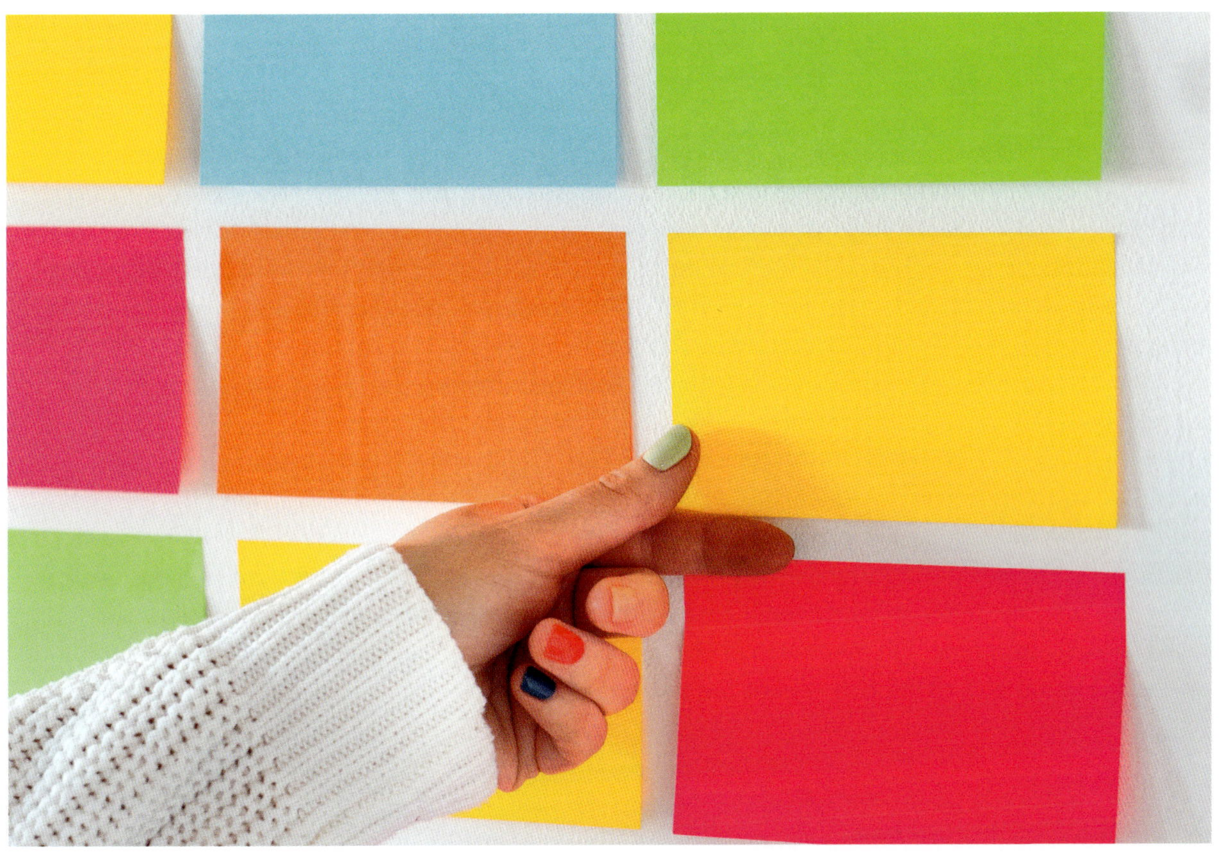

GETTING ORGANIZED AND REINVENTING THE LIST

For some creative people, the word *organized* is an instant turnoff, but there are ways to make it more fun and manageable. I'm a big fan of list making, but one giant list can feel so overwhelming that by the time you tick things off you find you're adding more to it. If I'm too busy thinking about the overall list, then I'm not present in that moment.

So what I suggest instead is to take a look at your list and write down the three to five most crucial things for the day (and remember to change the language you use!). Hide the larger to-do list, shove it behind a cushion, throw it to the other side of the room, and add each task to smaller sticky notes, or just one sticky note that you can recycle at the end of the day. The simple act of throwing it away can feel so fulfilling. Another option is to write the tasks digitally on your phone or computer and delete the document at the end of the day. Believe me, dragging it into the trash feels so good!

JAZZ IT UP AND REWARD YOURSELF

You've got to make the mundane tasks fun. Try using fun stationery like bright pink calculators or flamingo-shaped pens (or even making your own planners if you're a designer!). When taking a break in between tasks play your favorite song and dance around, or while you're waiting for the kettle to boil try some yoga poses or stretches. Have your favorite scented candle next to you, buy fresh flowers, change your screen saver to a motivational quote that really gets you going, add cute photos of favorite memories, wear your favorite feel-good outfit, and remember to keep reflecting on your vision board created in chapter 4, CLARITY. You should be in love with your creative ideas, so don't forget to nurture them, keep them feeling fresh, and stay loyal, just like the key attributes of any relationship!

I also try to give myself as many rewards as I can, whether it's a food treat, five minutes to myself, reading a book at lunchtime, or painting my nails. Breaking things up helps me get through those tasks and makes my day feel more exciting. Plan little rewards that help you celebrate your wins throughout the day. Planning lots of personal and social outings outside of work can also keep me really driven. On the days I'm meeting a friend for a movie or something with an exact start time, I'm much less likely to procrastinate knowing time is tight. Knowing I'll be rewarded at the end of the day makes me work so much harder and smarter.

Be as kind to yourself as you are to others.

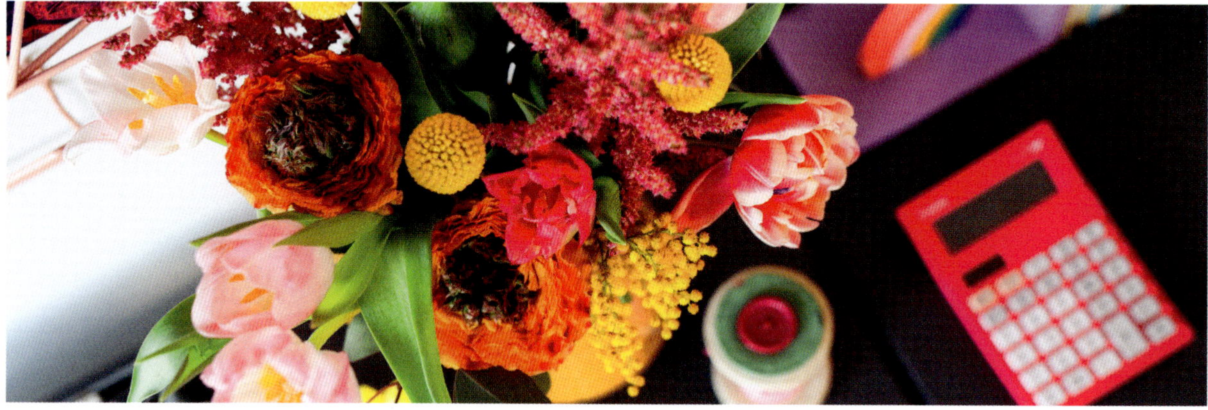

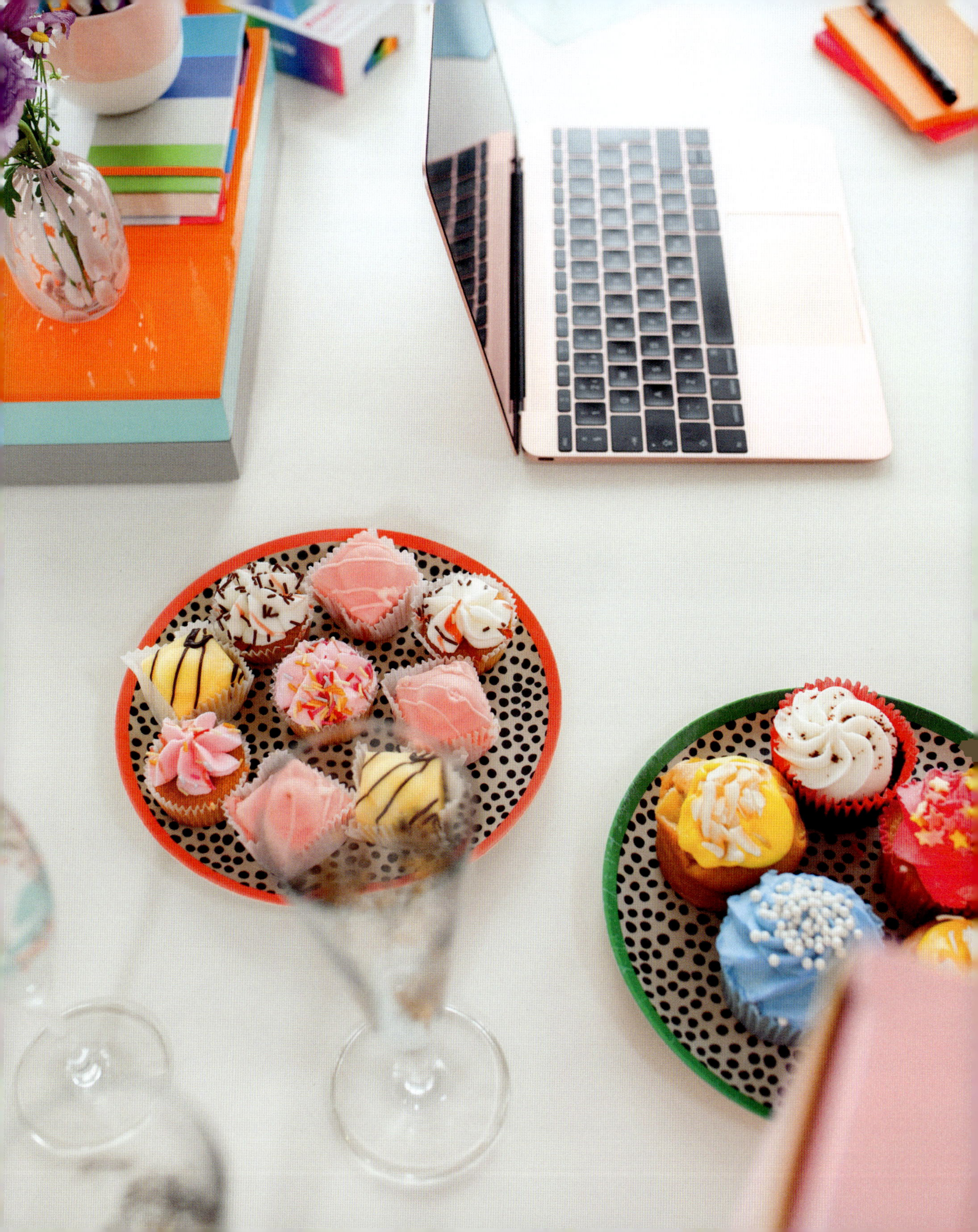

ASKING FOR HELP AND COMBATING ISOLATION

Don't be afraid to ask for help. I know we can't all have employees or a team, and when I was starting out, I didn't have any of that. I had to wear many hats and juggle many tasks. As this then gave me less time to rest, it would impact my energy levels and therefore my motivation and creative output. I'd ask kind family members and friends to help me with things such as studio organization, packing orders, or sewing. Even just asking for help from a partner or friend in preparing meals ahead of busy days, or help maintaining your home, can bring some relief. It's easy to feel like everything is on you, but trust me, as someone who's incredibly independent, it's not a sustainable way of living.

SHARED EXPERIENCE

One of my mentees, Catherine Worsley from the UK, came to me when she was feeling stuck and wanted to be more proactive.

"One thing that has stuck with me is how Rachael encouraged me to use positive visualization to make my goals seem more tangible. I also felt like I had someone amazing on my side, which for someone who works on their own is a real comfort. That approach obviously had an effect, because in the last year things have taken off for me in a way that I'd been dreaming about for a very long time! I was offered a short-term contract to design a whole new range of cards, then in the same week was signed by an illustration agency."

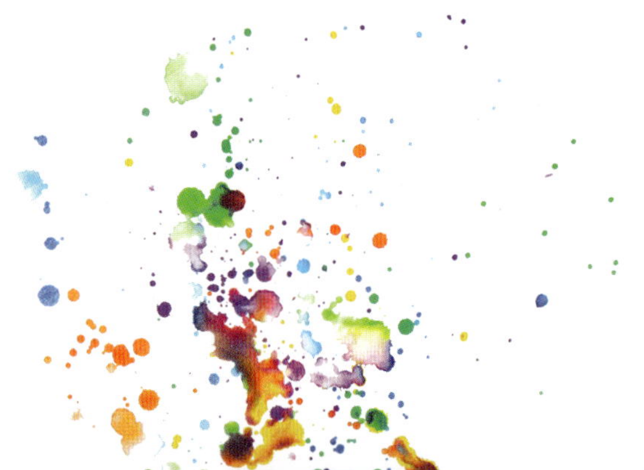

Getting help and rest is power not weakness.

Feeling isolated can be draining for a creative person. We can go into hermit mode really easily and begin to feel lost and agitated, drowning in a sense of loneliness or overwhelm. When I spot any of those feelings creeping in, I try to put on the brakes and do the simple things that make me feel less isolated, such as:

- Making a short phone call to hear another voice.
- Taking a proper break, whether it's sitting in the garden, reading a book, or getting out to a cafe for a change of scenery.
- Visiting a creatively inspiring place, whether it's once a week or once a month (schedule permitting) and commit to it.
- Going outside with my sketchbook, camera, or laptop.
- Networking with like-minded creatives, either in person or online.

Now jot down a few ways you can feel less lonely and isolated. For example, write in your diary, "Tuesday: take sketchbook to local museum and work on admin in the cafe" or "End of the month: meet with my artist group online." While I'm a fan of spontaneity, it's healthy to have plans and a routine to combat the factors that sap our creativity.

MAKE TIME FOR YOU—YOU'RE YOUR MOST VALUABLE ASSET

You need to protect your time. If you plan a day off, do as much as you can to make that time out of bounds. It's easier said than done sometimes, particularly when you've got a new idea and you're so excited about it. When I fall in love with an idea, I want to lock myself away and become a complete hermit and only work on that one thing. That can be fine in short bursts, but I've been known to commit to too much and feel stressed when other responsibilities come calling. Then what happens? I face burnout and start to feel resentful of the thing I was initially excited about because I'm now relating it to feeling ill or tired.

So this is me giving you permission, and me letting you know to give yourself permission, to take a break! Make fresh air and a change of scenery compulsory throughout your day. We're all guilty of not moving from our desk at times. Why not save that phone call you have to make and let it accompany you on a walk? Have some YOU time.

> Please respect your physical and mental health as much as your creativity. You can't pour from an empty cup!

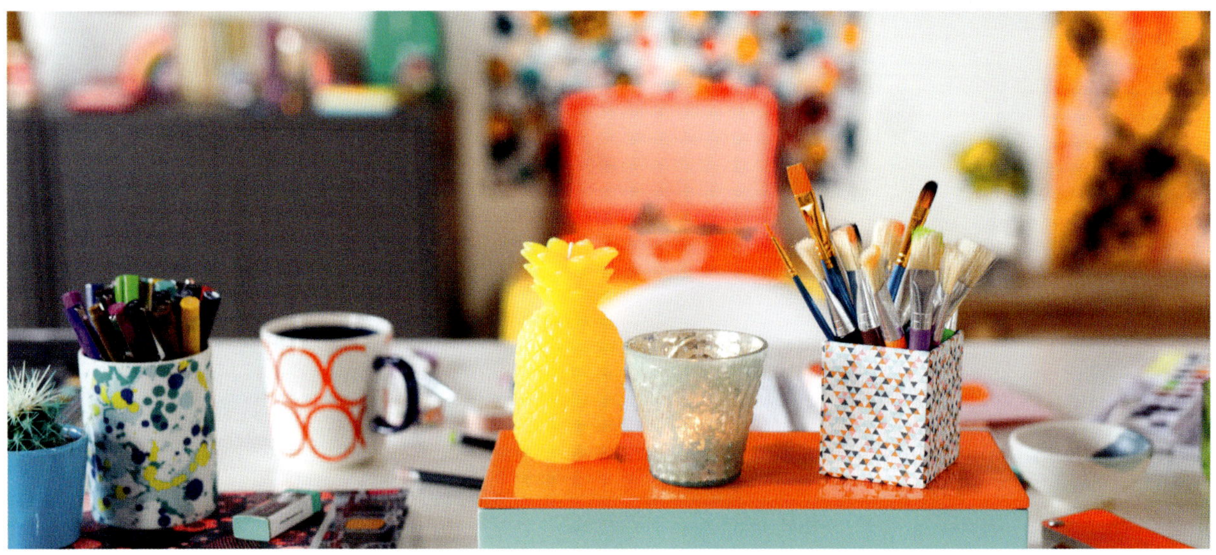

ASSESSING YOUR LIFESTYLE

Think about whether there is anything you can do to free up time so that you can focus on your creativity that little bit more. Can you offer to pick up someone else's child one day at school and then they do the school run in return for you? Can you do an online food shop? On a Sunday can you prepare your food for the week ahead, so that you're more organized and eating well? Sometimes making small sacrifices can also make a big impact. For example, if you watch two TV episodes a night, what happens if you scale it back to just one? Maybe your exercise time goes into the evening rather than the morning because you can do your project earlier on. Reevaluate what you can do, how you can fit it around your personal and professional lifestyle, and how you can make it work for you.

Also remember you can say "no" or "not right now." Are you being pulled in too many directions? Perhaps you feel bad if you don't volunteer to help in your community, at your child's school, or with a family member, so you find yourself saying yes to everything. All of those times you are saying yes you are sacrificing your own creative, personal, or work time, and each of those can stack up. Assess your routine and schedule, then mark out your creative time and protect it. Make that time non-negotiable, just as you would with a medical appointment; honor that time just the same. Mark your creative time in your diary or planner, block spaces in for the future, add it to your traditional paper diary or digital calendar, or stick it on the fridge—whatever and wherever works for you—but do not change it! That's your time to show up and work some of your creative magic.

It may sound silly initially, but try drafting three to five scenarios where you're likely to get asked to do something and practice saying "no" or "not now." Say the words out loud or jot them down in a notebook to really make them stick.

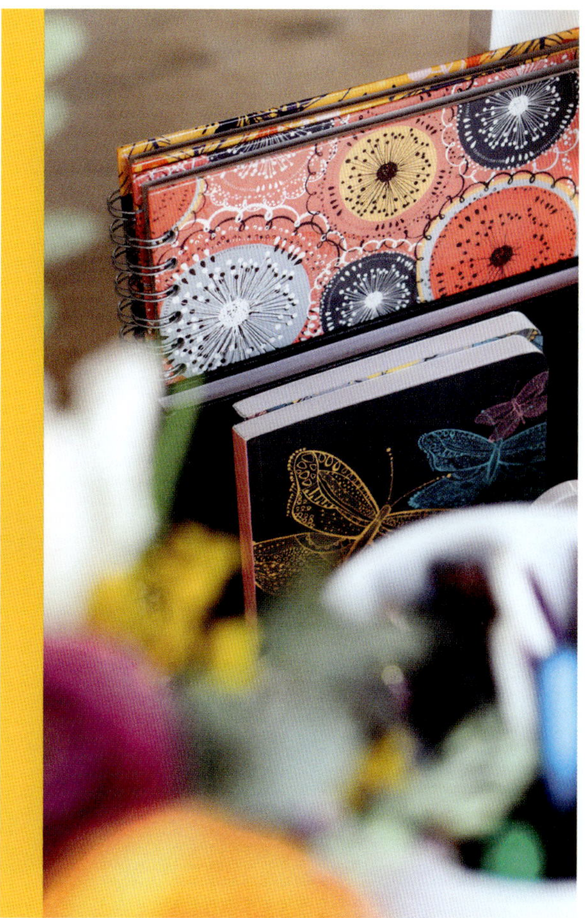

RECOGNIZE WHAT MOTIVATES YOU

For me, color is such a mood boost. If I'm feeling like I need some energy, wearing a color I love just does something to me; it really makes me create differently. Music is also important for my creative process; whether it's design work or life admin, there are certain playlists that I put on. I'll play acoustic music if I want to relax and concentrate. I have a few that are my go-to artists for when I'm just stressed, lost, or I need to feel calm. I'm also a big fan of listening to the radio. I have a little vintage-looking radio and there's just something about switching it on as I'm making a cup of tea, that feels like a comfort blanket.

Having a hot drink on my desk is a ritual for me. It might be simple, it might be bizarre, but I know I'm more likely to stay at my desk and complete the task before me if I have tea. However, I'm also one of these people who makes a cup of tea, then forgets about it and it goes cold because I get so engrossed in what I'm working on. A little tip I have is to switch to having these nice little vanilla chai teas because as they cool, they still taste quite nice!

So what works for you? What's going to motivate you to work your best? Make a list (in your own style) right here and now and pin it on the wall.

You are your only limit.

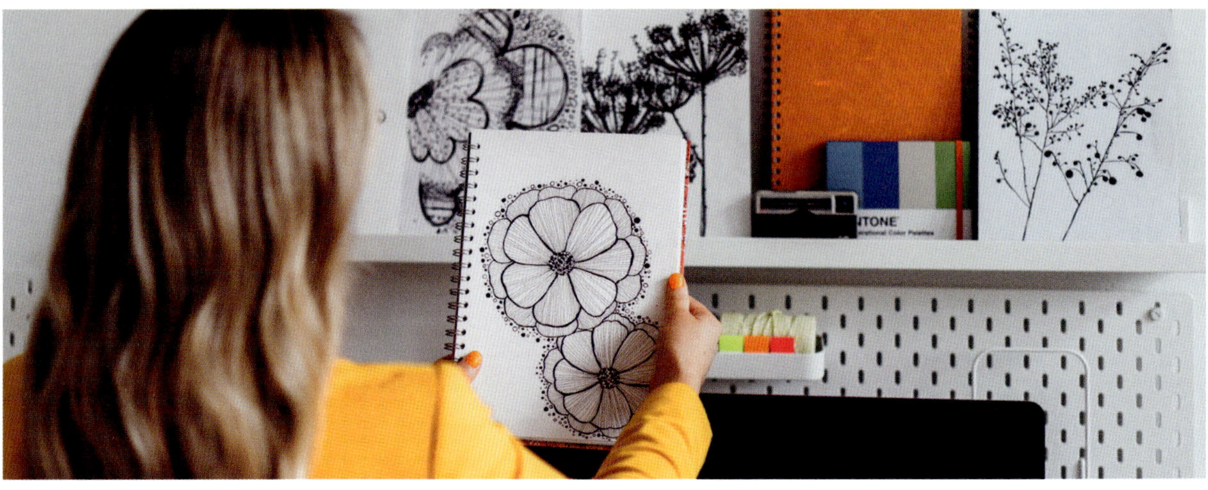

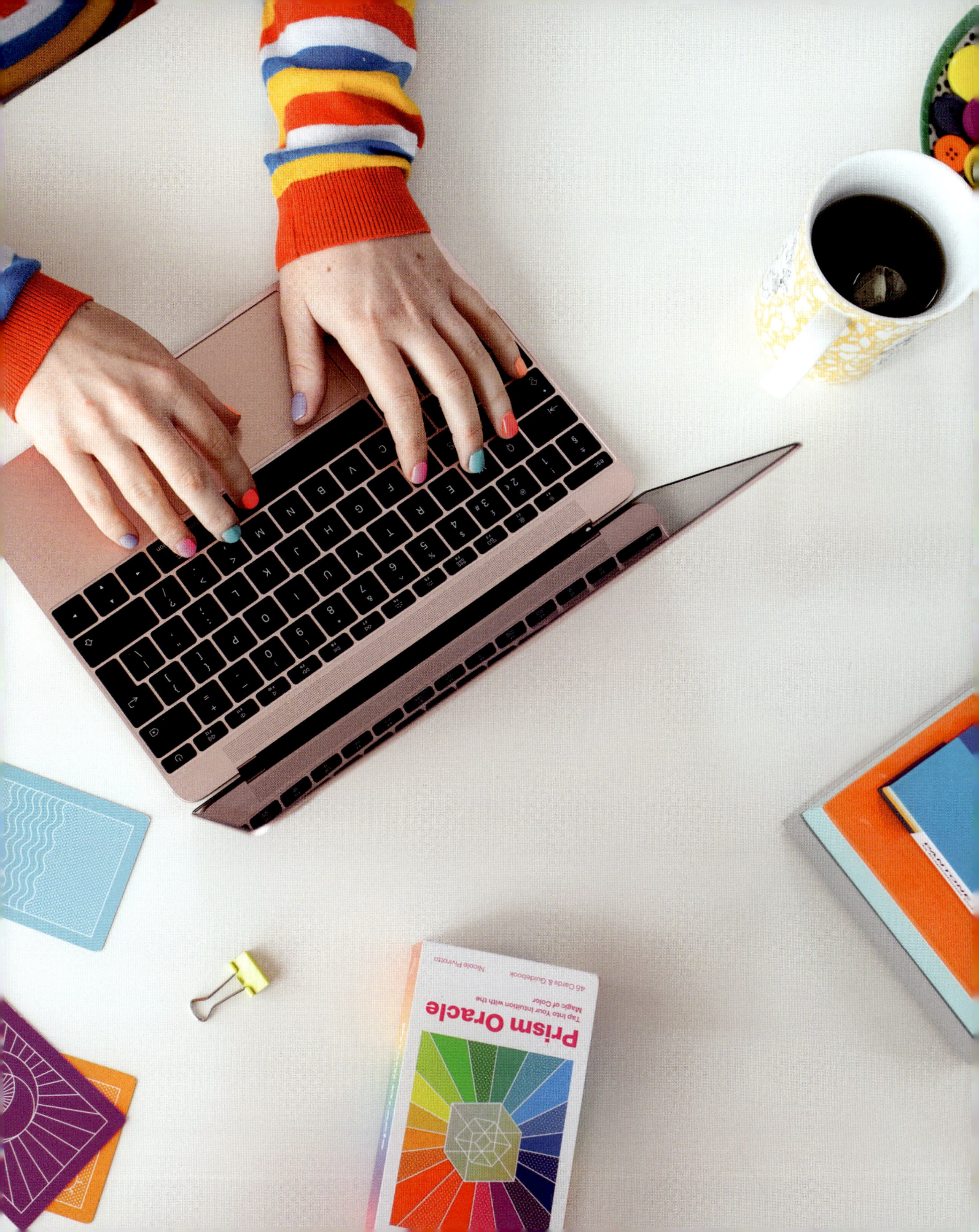
Prism Oracle
Tap Into Your Intuition with the Magic of Color
45 Cards & Guidebook
Nicole Piyrotto

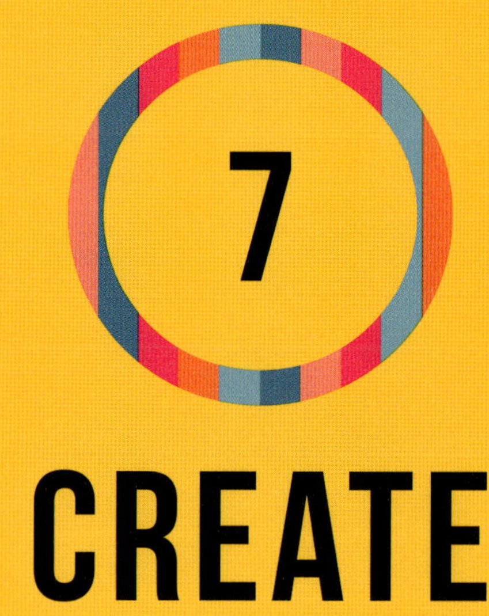

CREATE

How do I create with intention?

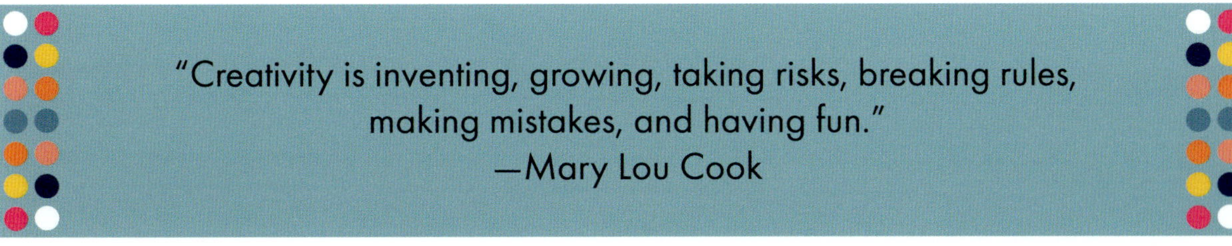

Creativity is a magical power we each hold within us. Even when you create something small, give yourself a pat on the back as you have been brave enough to create something for yourself or others. That in itself is a gift to the world and quite extraordinary.

We can all create as and when we feel like it, and I'm the biggest fan of making room for spontaneity and designing in an uncontrived way. However, if we understand what makes us truly happy and have clarity with our goals, we naturally create with a clearer purpose. Sometimes we can do this with an action plan, but a lot of the time when we have all the key ingredients together, we can create in what feels like an effortless and subconscious way.

In this chapter my goal is to help you create with more intention. I hope that as you have been working through the book you feel you have been on a journey of creative exploration and self-discovery too. You've understood what makes your soul shine in a way to light the rest of your wonderful journey.

THOUGHTS TO PONDER ON CREATIVITY

What they said:
"There are no career opportunities in art. You should do something else."

What happened:
Nearly two decades successfully working in the industry.

I think it's so important to take time to reflect on what we love about being creative. Say to yourself, "You know what, I'm a creative, how lucky am I to be a creative person?" Just think about how amazing it is to have been given this gift. Creativity is a blessing that we can sometimes take for granted.

I've lost count of the many times people have said things such as, "But that's not a *real* job, is it?" when I've told them about my work and aspirations. It's always said in a tone that implies that you can't make a living from your creativity or be deemed a successful person. Sure, the creative world can be competitive, and some people experience struggles (as do people in other industries), but gosh it's so rewarding and truly euphoric to get to do this. To those people, I remind them to look around themselves, *really look*. Everything around them has been touched by creativity, from the chair they sit on, to the socks they wear, to the notebook they use.

What a boring place the world would be without creatives! Sure, I'm not a surgeon saving lives, but creative work is still and always will be *important*. Creativity is incredibly powerful, and I will forever continue to celebrate that message through my own work and community.

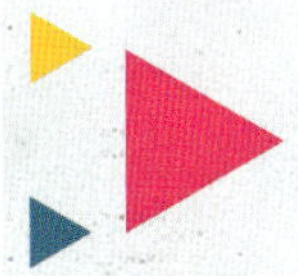

Create the work you want to attract.

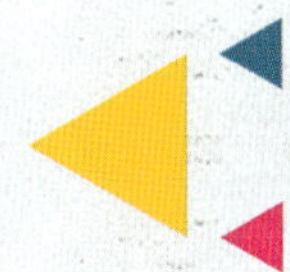

I have sworn by this throughout my whole career. Early on, after leaving my in-house design job, I wanted to avoid working on restricted designs, Christmas art, and limited color palettes, and stressing over genre and my customer base. I wanted to attract commissions for art that were playful, energetic, and bursting at the seams with color. So I carved out the time and began to create that kind of art, and it felt so liberating. That was when the type of client I wanted also began to take notice. By being clear on what you want to create, *you* set the tone for what will come your way.

SHARED EXPERIENCE

One of my clients, Vibeke Larsen from Norway, has been a designer for many years but came to me when she was struggling to find her own creative style.

"Rachael advised me to value my talent and the experience I already had and be proud of it. To cultivate 'my youniqueness,' and have confidence that my work is good enough. That made me see how much I have developed the 'true me' already. I have worked on developing my own style through 'me time' and creating just to create. I've become more aware of what and who I want to design for, and how to 'target' my work through social media and my portfolio. I am now prouder of what I do and I've increased my self-confidence. I have also gained more confidence in taking steps outside my comfort zone."

CREATE AND EXPLORE VARIOUS SUBJECT MATTER

When approaching difficult subjects or ideas outside of your comfort zone, there are several ways you can break down the creative barriers that can at first seem overwhelming.

You can try to write down the descriptive terms that come to mind when you think of the theme you are working with. For example, for "geometric," think "mathematical," "ordered," "regimented," "hexagon," "stripe," etc. This method can be as effective with any media from photography to music. The point of this exercise is to look and approach subject matter in a different way that can resonate with you.

Expanding your range of subject matter opens up new audiences, clients, and markets for your work, so it's a vital part of growing your creative skills. Just don't forget to have fun with it! It really is true—practice makes perfect (although I don't believe in "perfect" and believe *there are no mistakes*). The possibilities for subject matter are endless.

When trying new things, try creating a number of versions to loosen you up, zooming in for detail and zooming out for a different perspective. Look up, look down. Flip it, reflect it, rotate it. The more you are willing to adapt and push your boundaries, the more things will become less daunting over time. Continuing to try out new ideas is a fantastic way to expand your comfort zone and strengthen your creative muscles.

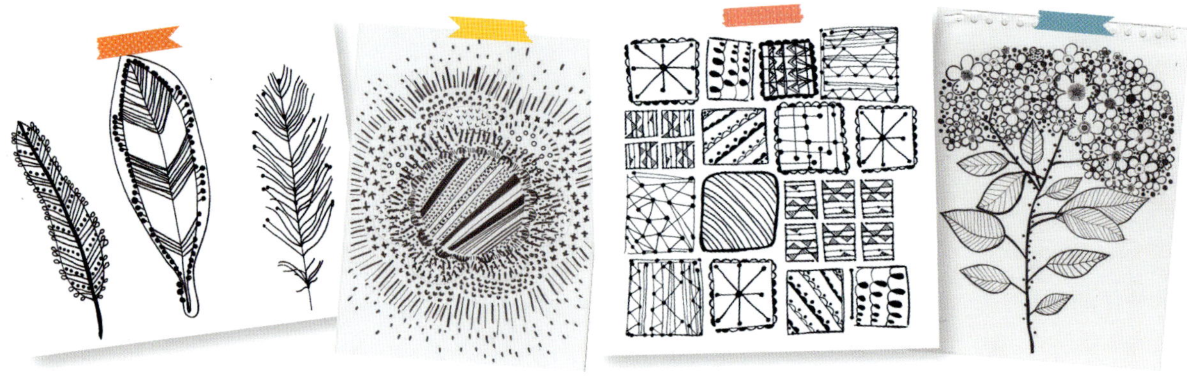

CREATE WHAT YOU LIKE AND DISLIKE

It's inevitable that there will be certain subject matters you love to work with and go back to time and time again. There will also be subjects that you find challenging to create. It is important to explore new options while allowing your signature creative style to shine through. I truly believe that the most successful creatives (whose careers have longevity) are the ones who are willing to adapt, change, mix it up, broaden their horizons, naturally evolve, and face new challenges head-on.

With that in mind, I want you to list the five things you find *easiest* to draw. Here is my list:

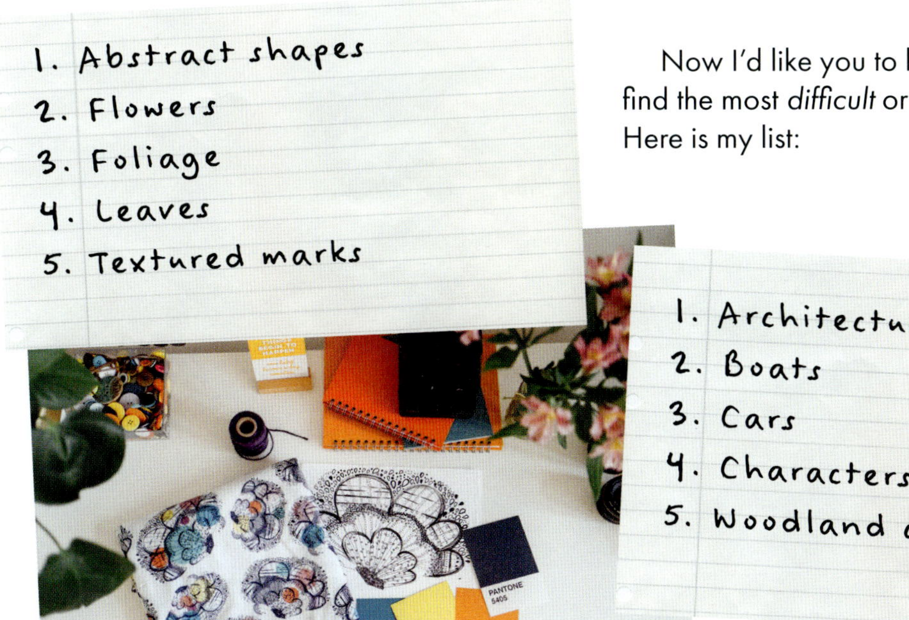

Now I'd like you to list the five things you find the most *difficult* or *can't imagine* drawing. Here is my list:

1. Architecture
2. Boats
3. Cars
4. Characters
5. Woodland creatures

Now open up your notebook or sketchbook or grab some paper and draw one item from each of the above lists each day for the next few weeks (yes, that includes the things you can't ever imagine drawing!). Set aside ten minutes each day, whether first thing in the morning with your coffee break or later in the evening in front of the TV, and work with these items. Tick them off from your lists as you go along and see how many new pieces you can come up with! You never know where this might lead as you discover new ways of creating and looking at the things you think you dislike or felt like you couldn't approach.

REVISIT, ADAPT, AND MONETIZE EXISTING CREATIONS

As creatives, we have the natural urge to keep creating. That in itself is a gift. However, at times I have created endlessly, producing a mountain of drawings that I never get time to make into prints and patterns. Or I've created finished designs as personal pieces, but they have sat on my computer when I should really send them to my own client database or my agent.

I encourage you to allocate time to past creations that may not have seen the light of day, or pieces with great potential that with a little refresh can be something quite spectacular. This has personally worked for me over the years, financially through a new income stream, and creatively as it has given me more freedom to experiment with other projects. I always encourage this with my design school community, because once someone licenses or sells something they already made, they realize the worth of their creations and that perhaps they are sitting on a pot of gold.

Do you have photography archives you can revisit, hard drives with existing designs, or full sketchbooks that are hiding away and have never seen the light of day? Sometimes time (or the lack of) can play a huge part in whether our creations are shared with the world or in fact another soul. These creations are a part of you, and naturally some of our creative work will be better than others, but if you never share it, how do you know it's not something someone else will love or something you can monetize?

Select five things that you are going to reuse, repurpose, or finish and get them out there! Here's my list:

1. Complete a butterfly drawing (I will only purposely draw half of a butterfly, as I prefer to complete it on the computer, making the symmetry much easier).
2. Dig out a Chinese lantern design I started ages ago and never finished.
3. Curate a group of existing Cuba travel photos to influence my next piece.
4. Design a piece of art combining both mine and my son's art (something I've been promising him for a while).
5. Re-color an existing design inspired by the latest Pantone Color of the Year.

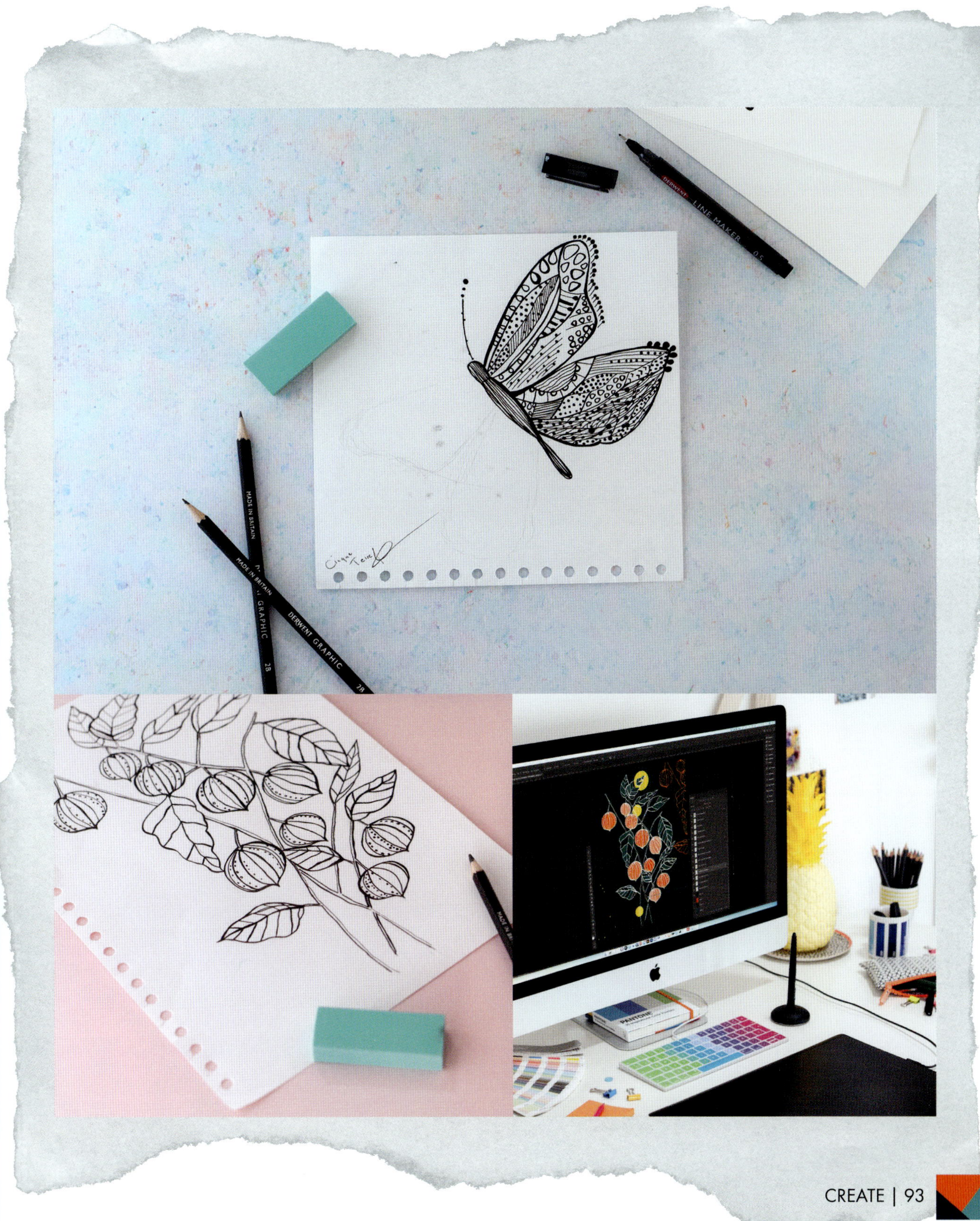
DERWENT
LINE MAKER 0.5
MADE IN BRITAIN
DERWENT GRAPHIC
2B
PANTONE

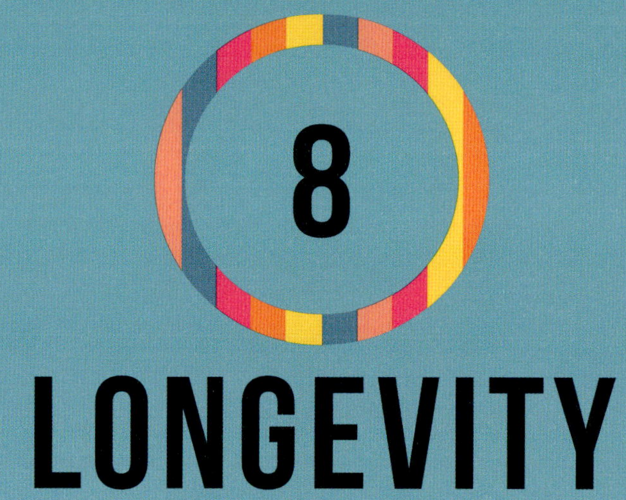

8 LONGEVITY

How can I achieve creative longevity?

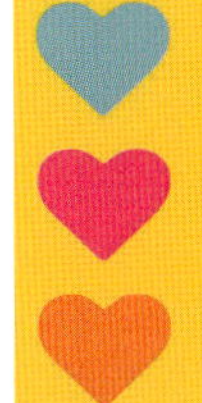

"Do what you love, and you'll never work a day in your life."
—Confucius

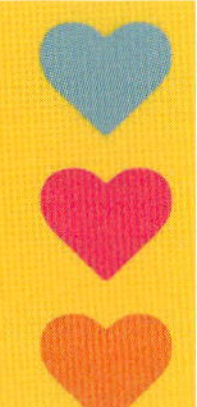

As creatives, we can overanalyze and worry even when things are going well. We can have that moment of doubt creep in and think, "But how long will my art be popular?" or "Will they move on to the next trend or upcoming designer?" To have longevity in anything it's important to recognize that life happens and the pace of your creative work will need to reflect that. I'm known for great output levels and putting in extra hours, and while that's great at times to get projects off the ground, it's not always sustainable. In recent years, while navigating a new way for my personal life, I've had to pull back on certain things.

We need to avoid burnout and nurture our souls so that we can put our energy into what we do best. While we can't control the ebbs and flows in life, there are a number of things we can do to have more creative control over our success and keep our creativity flowing for a long time to come.

THOUGHTS TO PONDER ON LONGEVITY

Often we worry about running out of ideas, especially when we get a total block. The beauty of our creative talents is that they were given to us to be explored, shared, and celebrated in whichever form that may take us, whether as a hobby or an income stream. We just need to know when to move forward, pause, evaluate, seek new inspiration, and power through.

Exploring who I am as a creative and becoming comfortable with myself and my process allows me to shine in my work. I also say to my community, "Inject you into every design." But it goes beyond that because injecting you into *everything* you do is your superpower.

I always think about the full process, from the emails I send, to the designs I create, to my finished products. How do I make people feel and what will they remember me for?

I want them to know who I am, feel energized and uplifted, and feel they've received a fun yet professional approach. If your energy and passion shine through, people will feel it and want to receive it.

> "You can't use up creativity;
> the more you have, the more you use."
> —Mary Angelou

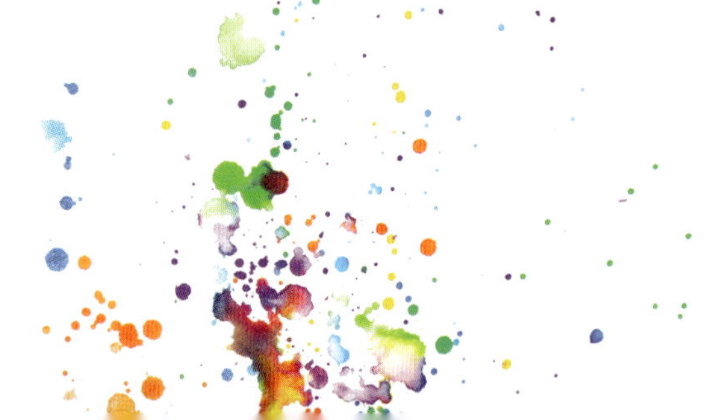

CREATIVE EXERCISES

MAKING A CONNECTION

Professional etiquette can go a long way. Treat people how you expect to be treated and never rush opportunities or act in haste. I love the saying "You never get a second chance to make a first impression." While the creative industry is huge, at the same time it can feel close-knit. A large percentage of my income comes from word of mouth, and I'm the type of person that really does share. If I can't take on a commission, I'll recommend someone I know or share a job or competition opportunity; while I don't do these things to get anything in return, my clients remember me for assisting them when I didn't have to, and often they'll do the same for me.

So the next time you get an email or a direct message ping asking for help or wanting to connect, what would happen if instead of ignoring or deleting it, you took five minutes to respond? Wouldn't it feel so good to help? What else might come from it? What kind of connection could you make for the future? Or if there are hectic times and you simply can't respond, why not set up an FAQ section on your website or have an automated reply with useful links to previous interviews?

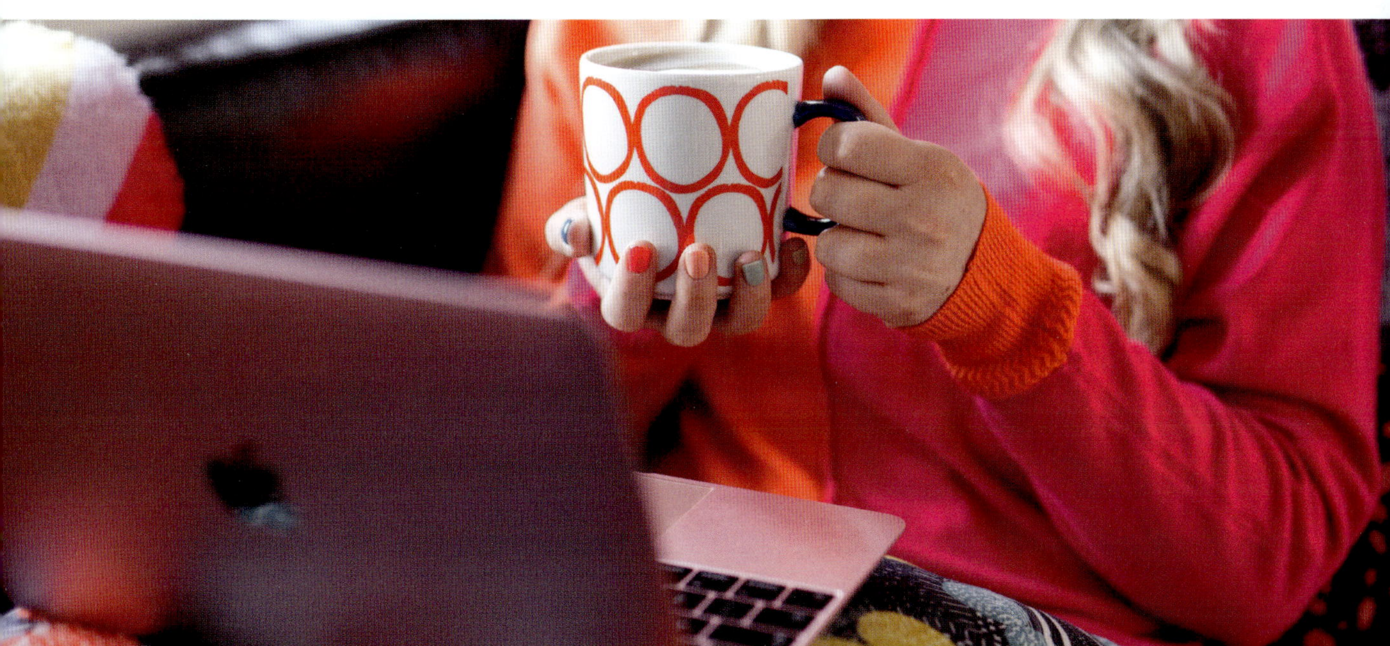

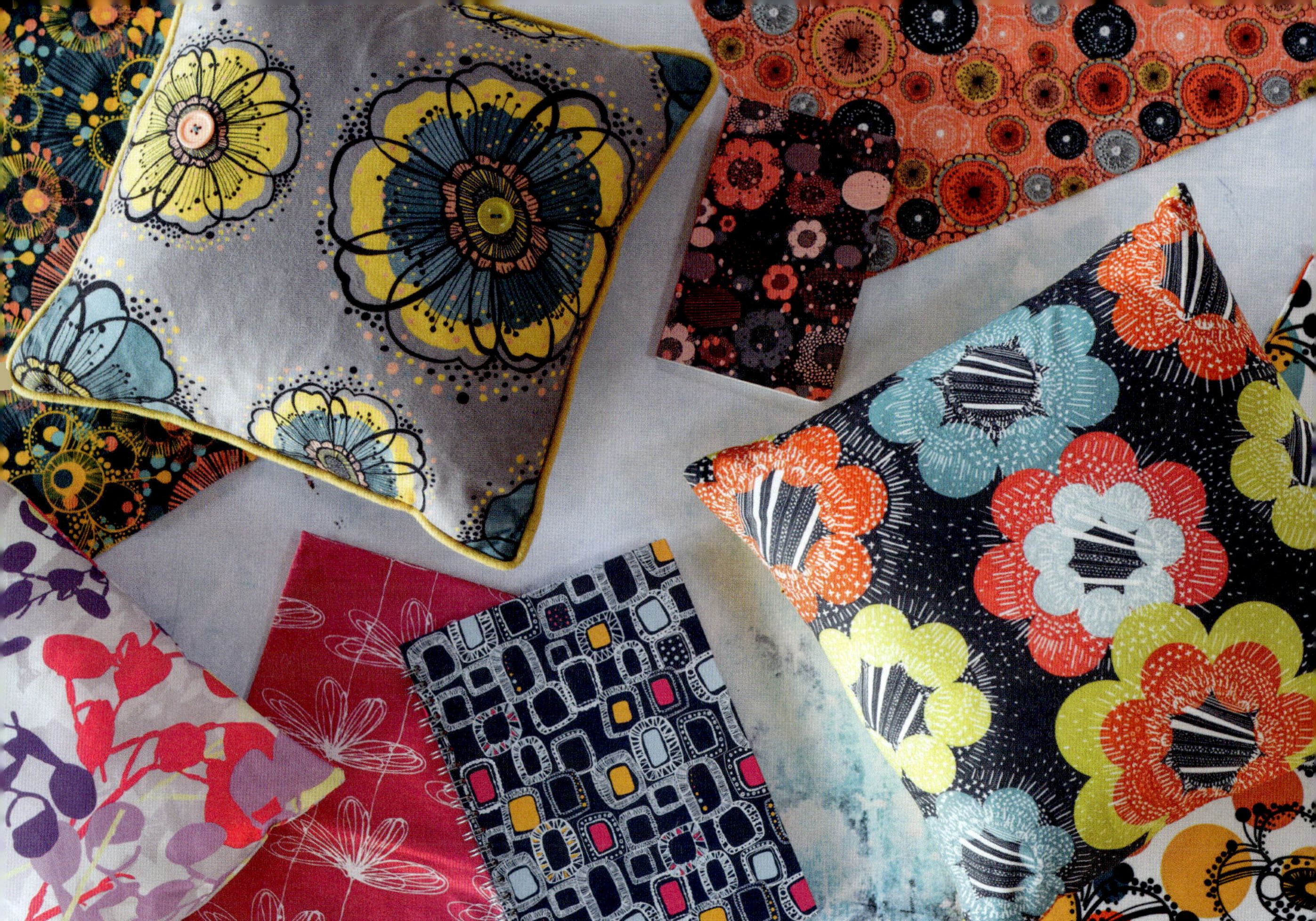

EXPLORING OPPORTUNITIES

There's such a broad scope of opportunities for creatives that allow us to flourish: from licensing art to manufacturing products, from personalized art to company commissions, from writing and teaching to workshops and online classes. Then there are the multiple markets and audiences we can tap into. Although endless possibilities can be overwhelming at times, I like to flip my reaction and think, "Wow, I get to choose from so many different things. Creativity really is abundant."

If you haven't done so already, write a list of products, projects, or kinds of work that you've always wanted to try. Rather than feeling overwhelmed at how many things you want to do, marvel at the options and amazing opportunities you have.

LEARNING NEW THINGS

In our forever changing creative industry it can feel daunting at times to keep up with new techniques and software advances; there will always be so much to explore. Rather than feeling overwhelmed, try to be excited about the fact that our creative world never stands still. There are so many opportunities that we can never possibly feel bored. It's important to keep up with new developments to not fall behind the times, but never let this make you feel inadequate or that your current process is outdated. Chip away at the learning and use it to complement what you already do. If you feel like you are ready for a new skill to shake up your world, then by all means explore that. Our time is limited and so precious, and while we can't control many outside factors in this world, we can shape our creativity so that it leads to luminous longevity.

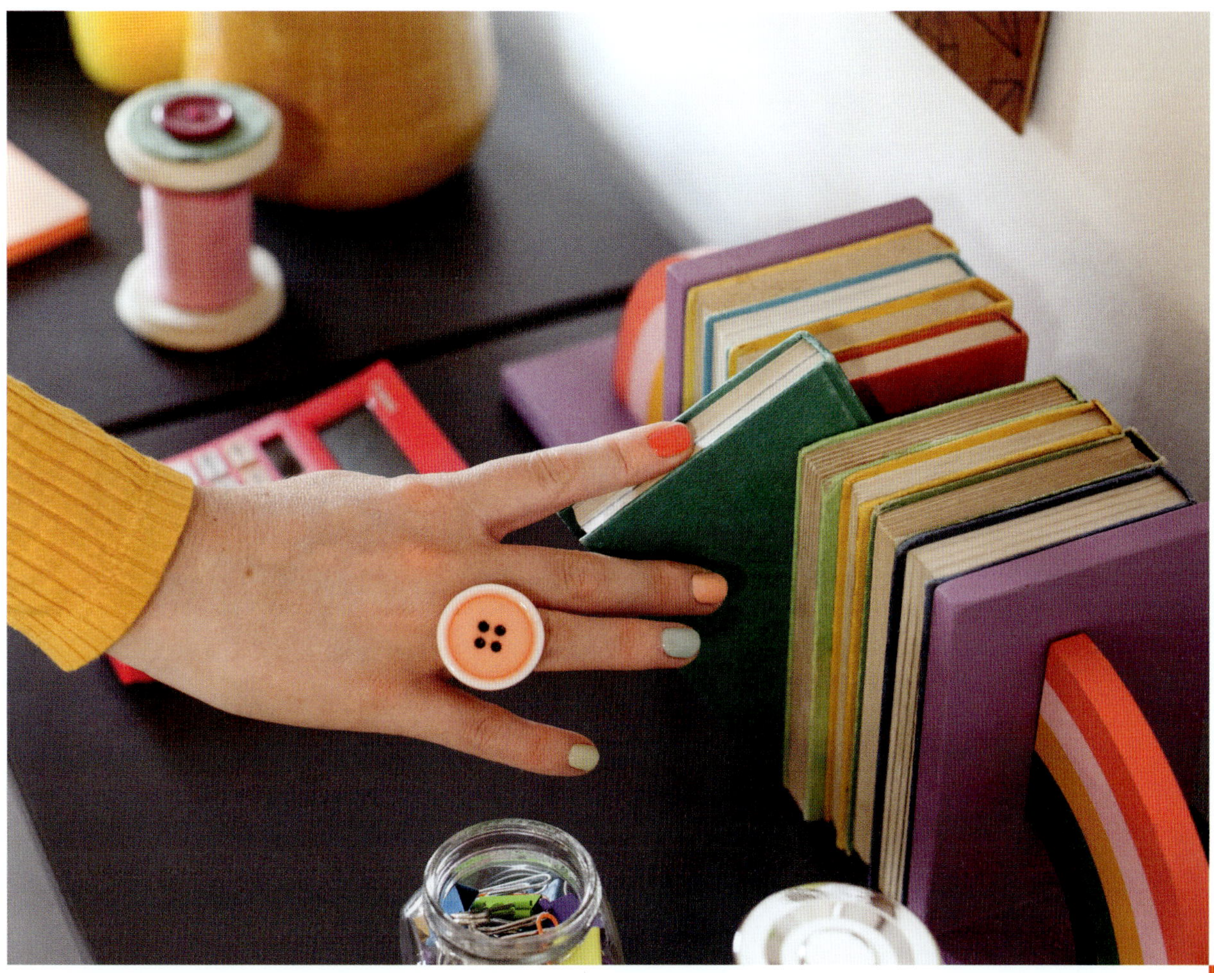

DIVERSIFY

It's important to not always rely on one income stream or focus on a single project. While that might be a great idea at certain times, particularly if you need to give something lots of attention to make it work long term, it can add pressure to get that one thing right.

It doesn't mean you have to work in lots of areas (as I do), but diversifying the area you are in can really bring something new to the table. For example, if you sell products and rely on Instagram to generate all your sales, why not open your own website shop, or join a platform like Etsy? Not only does this bring in a new audience, but it also gives you peace of mind to not be reliant on one income source.

If you work on regular client commissions, be sure to have a number of regular clients and don't be afraid to take on new ones. Sometimes we are afraid of rocking the boat if we try to fix what's not already broken. However, there have been times in my career when I've had an ongoing gig that's paid me decently, was enjoyable, and felt mostly relaxed and comfortable, and then out of nowhere the company had huge budget cuts or sadly even closed and the work dried up. I've never admitted this out loud before, but when I was once going through some financial pressure, I was approached for some in-house art direction work for a pretty cool and well-paid, full time job with lots of travel. I did think about taking it for a fleeting moment because I was feeling insecure in my own work, but deep down I knew I didn't want to do it and that I'd never give up on the two wonderful companies that I'd already helped build. Needing to feel secure can really impact our creativity in many ways, but don't let it cloud or affect your judgment so much that it could potentially shorten the life span of your creative journey.

When you read the word *diversify*, what immediately comes to mind? In what ways could you diversify what you offer? Are there some things on your goal list that you haven't tried yet? Pick one, give it a try, and see what can come from it.

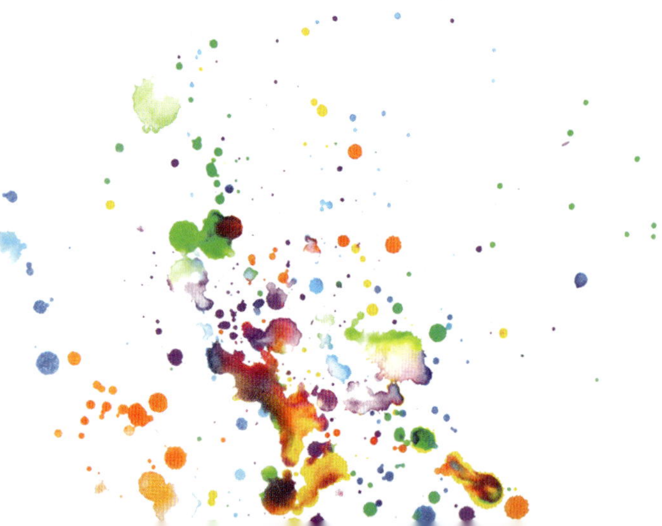

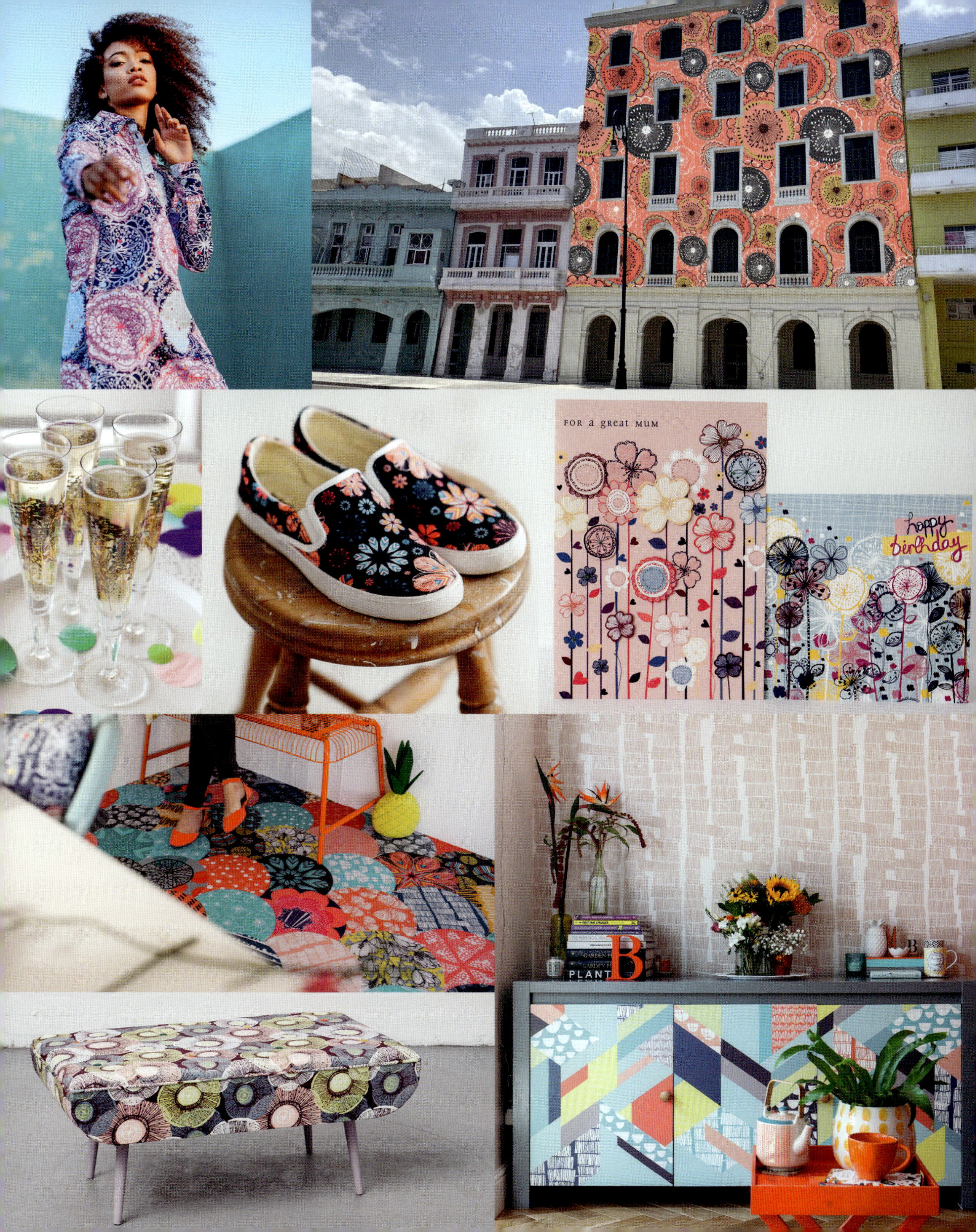
FOR a great MUM
happy birthday
PLANT

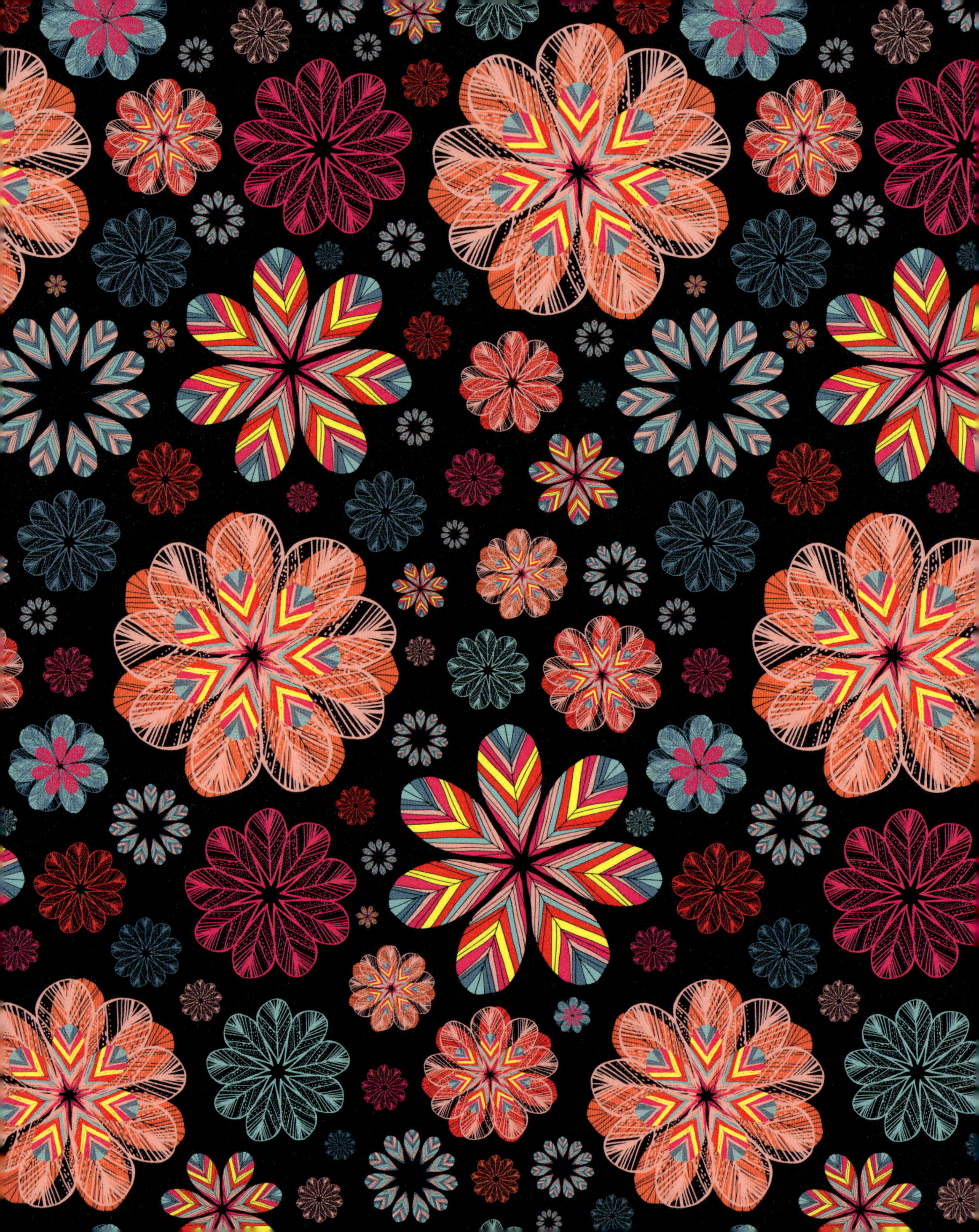

GIVE YOURSELF THE CREATIVE FREEDOM TO BLOOM

Planning ahead to help you achieve future goals is wonderful, but I must stress to leave a little room for freedom. If your structure is so tight that you are putting a restrictive vibe out there, you'll naturally close yourself off to opportunities that you might not have thought possible. I can honestly say that some of my career highlights have occurred during unplanned and unexpected moments.

Not doing the same thing year after year, even if it is bringing you great success, is so important, as at any time things can change. As creatives, we can become bored and restless if there's too much repetition. Thanks to giving myself more creative freedom, I would now describe myself as a multidisciplinary creative. It wasn't something that was planned, and it's been a very organic process that I'm glad I welcomed. Now I'm so grateful for every opportunity and experience.

Keep striving and streamlining your creative work, and reflect on other factors, such as your surroundings and workspace. Keep networking, learning, and growing.

Keep yourself fresh and inspired and keep nurturing all of the ingredients that will allow you and your creativity to bloom. Remember that flowers don't bloom all year and that magic also happens in the downtimes. Each flower blooms differently, and that's a part of what makes the process so beautiful.

Now would be an excellent time to check back on your clarity list (if you skipped this, flip back to chapter 4, CLARITY). Does your work make your heart sing? Are you making what you truly want to make? Does it feel like you and what your creative self really want? Are you owning who you are? I encourage you to do this check-in every three months or so and really dive into how your current creative work makes you feel.

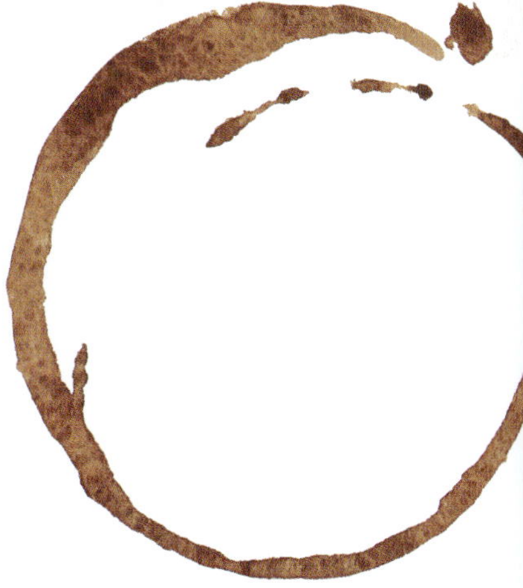

9

DESTINATION

I've reached my destination. What now?

> "Life is a journey, not a destination."
> —Ralph Waldo Emerson

Getting to your destination is one thing, knowing what's next is another. Throughout this book we've worked through themes such as clarity and motivation to help you get to your end creative goal, but sometimes when we reach that destination it can bring a mixture of feelings and even uncertainty for the next step. Perhaps we realize that the destination is not what we thought it would be or it has exceeded our every expectation.

Stop right now, pause, and soak it all in. Remember that there was once a time when you dreamed of being where you are now. We tend to always rush toward what's next, but I urge you to bask in the beauty of the now. This very moment is all yours.

I also want to take a moment to remind you that no one else can create exactly like you and that will always be your superpower, so whatever you turn your hand to, always have faith in your own magic.

While everyone reading this book is completely individual, as creatives it's apparent that we continue to share many of the same doubts, fears, and stumbling blocks with our process. Remind yourself, whether you've reached your destination, are worrying about the next thing, or are only at the start of your journey, that doubt and worry are shared experiences and you are not alone. These common themes and struggles will continue throughout your creative life, but if you know how to work with them, you can become a champion of powering up your creativity.

THOUGHTS TO PONDER ON DESTINATION

It might just be that you're reading this book and you are in fact at your destination, or it's the place you thought you wanted to be and when you got there it felt more like a disappointment or an anticlimax. That's okay, and it's okay to change or pivot from your original goal or idea. I've been there too and so have many of the thousands of creatives whom I've taught, engaged with, or individually mentored.

I encourage you to choose happiness every single time and follow your instincts, as they have gotten you this far. Sometimes we are so afraid to change or move the goalpost in fear of seeming unprofessional, unpredictable, or even greedy or selfish. Just because something was once the perfect dream doesn't mean you can't change your mind. Gosh, it really is as simple as moving or changing direction, it's really not that controversial. Often we are conditioned to follow the status quo and not dip outside of it, but we can design our own creative life, and why not?

Life is for making choices, choices that will nurture your current goal and destination, but if your heart is pulling you in a different direction, you are just as deserving to nurture new ideas.

It's okay to have more than one finish line.

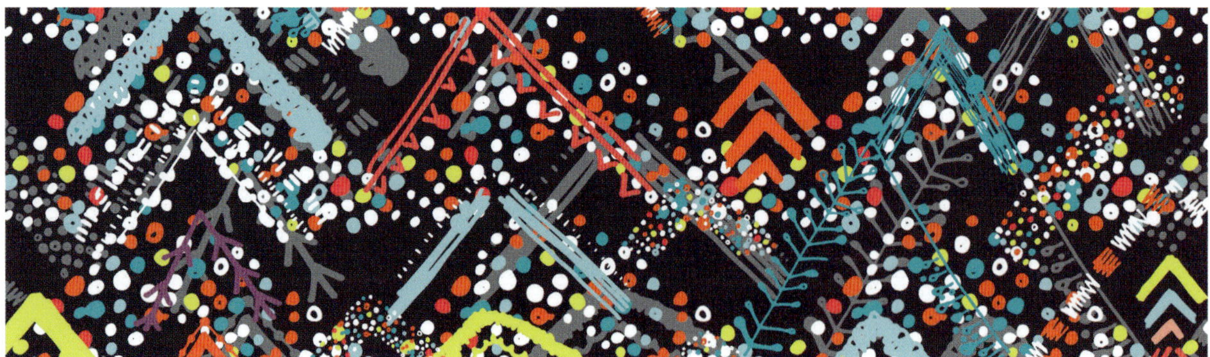

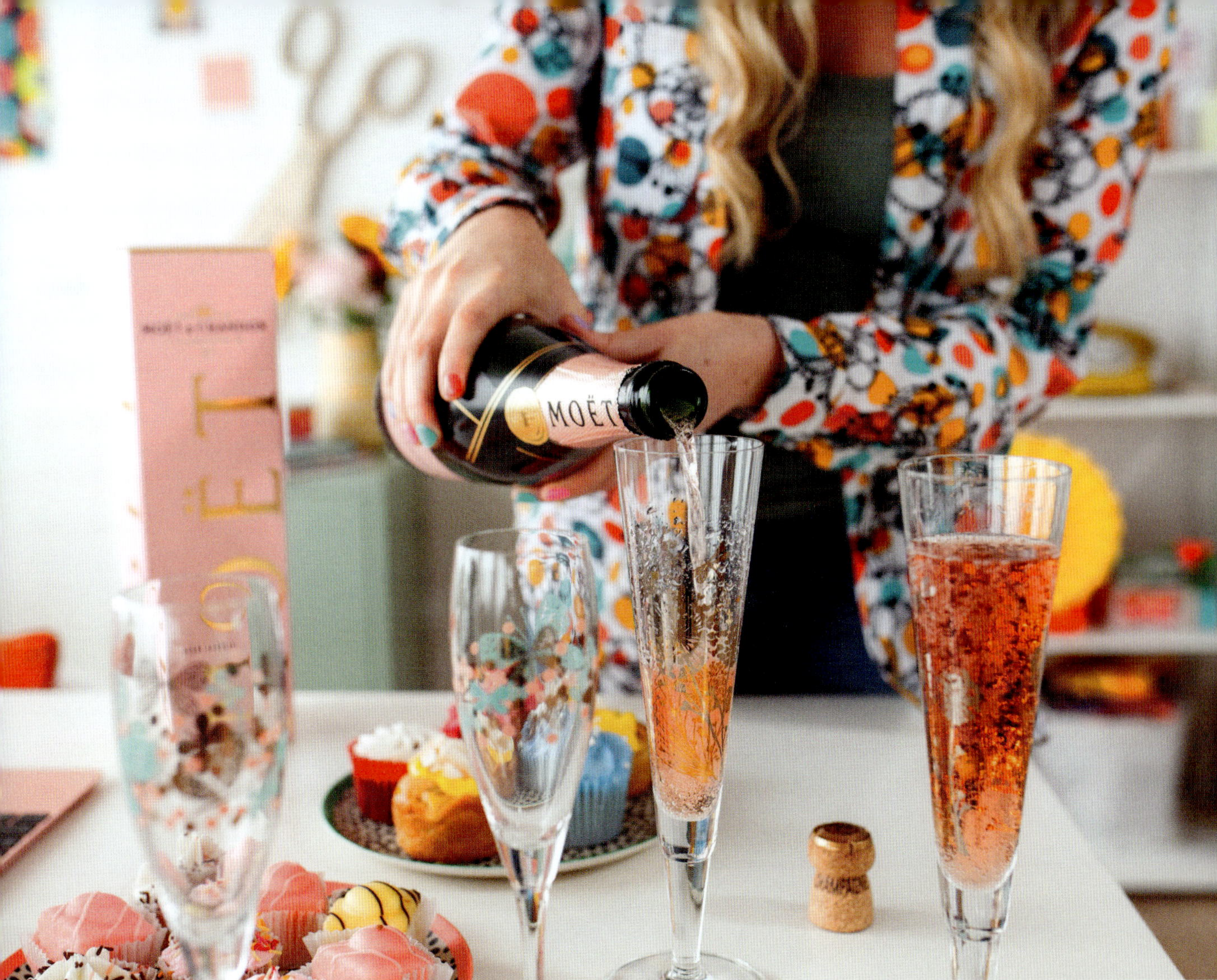

Now I also want you to learn to ***celebrate***. Once you have reached your destination or certain points in your creative journey, be sure to mark the occasion and take some time to reflect. I like to book something fun in my calendar, as it definitely spurs me on when I know a deadline is coming. Sometimes it's a spa day with a loved one, or just a day to myself reading a book. I like having things to look forward to. I've got the champagne waiting and I'm going to toast how I've done no matter the outcome.

On those hard days when you just feel like "Oh, what is going on? I can't do this," thinking about the little wins along the way can be a real pick-me-up. Whether it's something simple like a card a customer has sent you or a lovely review they've left, have these things around you. It's really important to cherish and celebrate magical moments like these no matter how small.

CREATIVE EXERCISES

TIME TO EVALUATE

It can be hard to comprehend a plan not working out, especially when we ticked every box and worked hard for it. But don't despair, right now is an important time to evaluate. Here are some questions I often ask myself when I've reached a destination:

- How does it make me feel?
- What did it add to my creativity?
- Has it improved or complemented my lifestyle?
- Have I enjoyed it?
- Is it sustainable?
- Am I content with the progress I made?
- Is there a set time frame or will it need to continue and keep evolving?
- Do I want to grow the idea or adapt it?

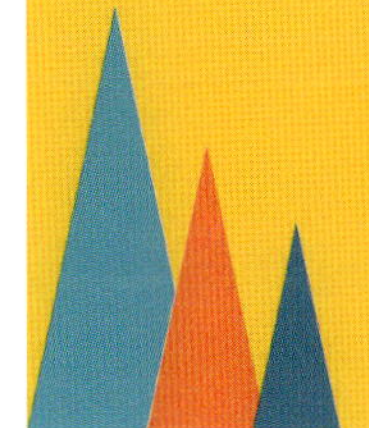

You will reach your destination
even though you travel slowly.
—Icelandic proverb

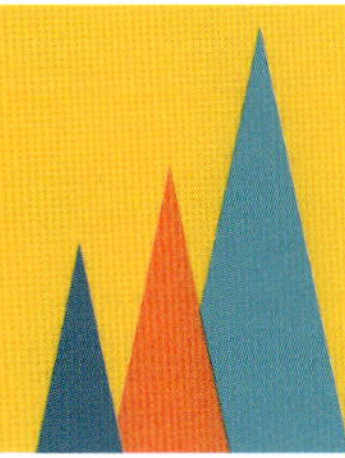

If I'm feeling lost with where I'm at or my next destination, I might ask myself:

- Am I happy with where I am?
- Was there anything that stressed me out?
- Did I perform as expected?
- What made me procrastinate?
- What didn't go to plan?

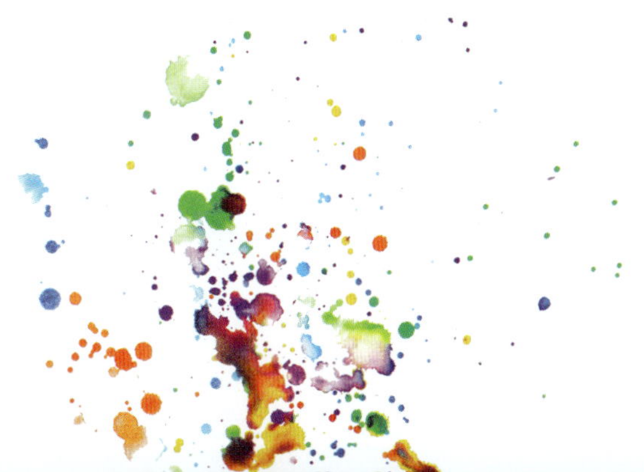

Another important question to ask on both lists is "What could I do better?" However, I want you to ask yourself that kindly, and remember to pat yourself on the back for having the courage to go after your dreams in the first place, and for reaching your destination at all. If you're reading this and you're not at your destination yet, don't worry, it'll happen—I have every faith in you. I often feel super happy with a creation or for finishing a project, but then later overanalyze it and literally pull it or myself apart. Over the years I've become better at being kinder to myself. Even when things go wrong, we can find the good in the little things, whether it's from learning something new or having the courage to push through.

In this creative exercise if you opted to fill out the second list, I urge you to make an additional list and look for the magic in what you did. Even if something didn't go to plan, there will be at least small achievements and skills learned along the way that you should celebrate.

MAGIC BOX

When I receive things like a wonderful customer review or letter, I keep it in a cute little "magic box." On hard days, I pull them out and they can be so uplifting. They remind me why I am where I am and why I need to continue to share my light and creativity with the world.

Take some time out in your day to collect those items, soak up those words, look at those photos, and pat yourself on the back—you did that! Often when we reach our destination, we can let it pass us by in a fleeting moment. This is a lovely exercise for practicing gratitude. Life is often busy for many of us, but moments like these can ground us and are so important.

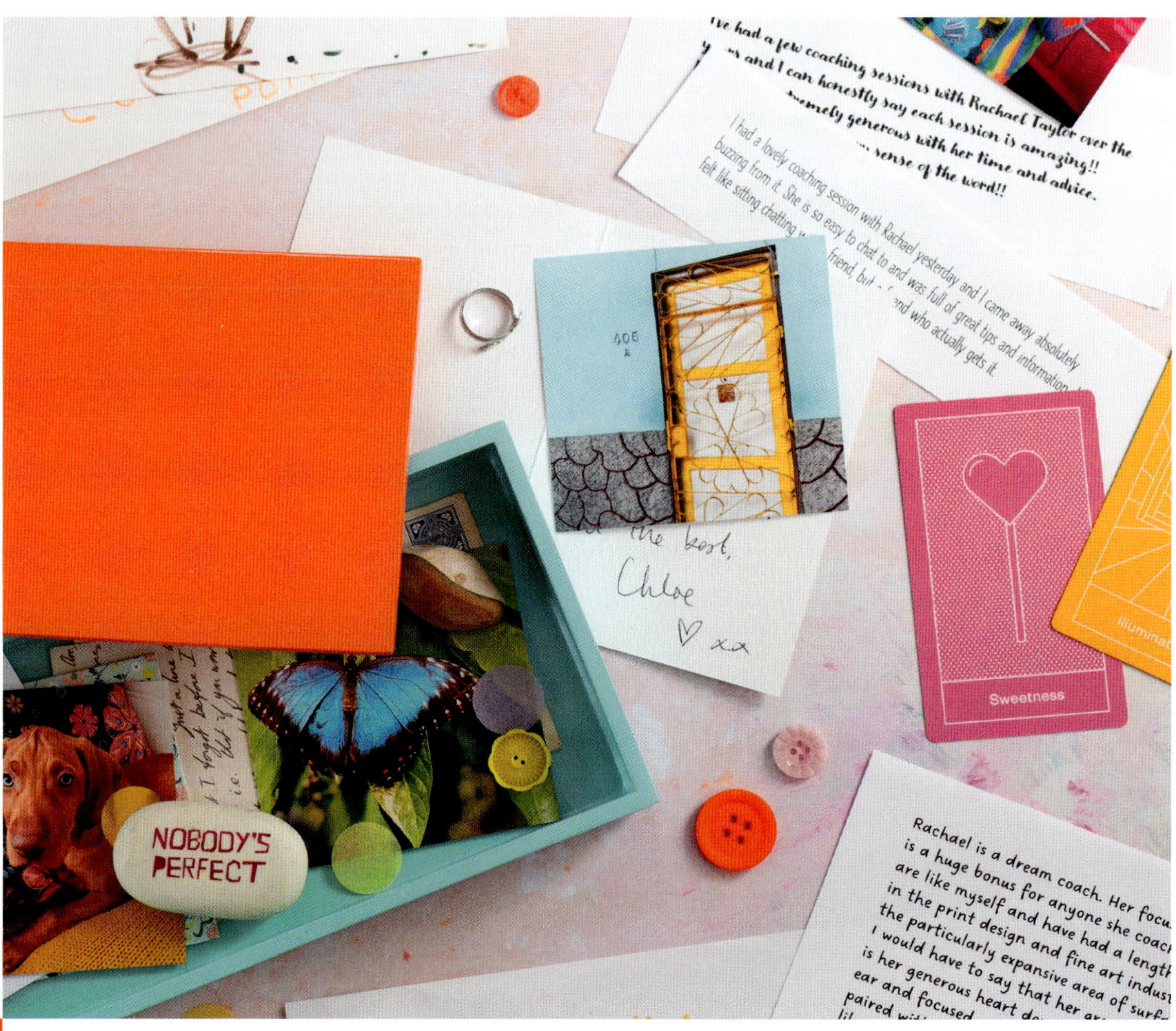

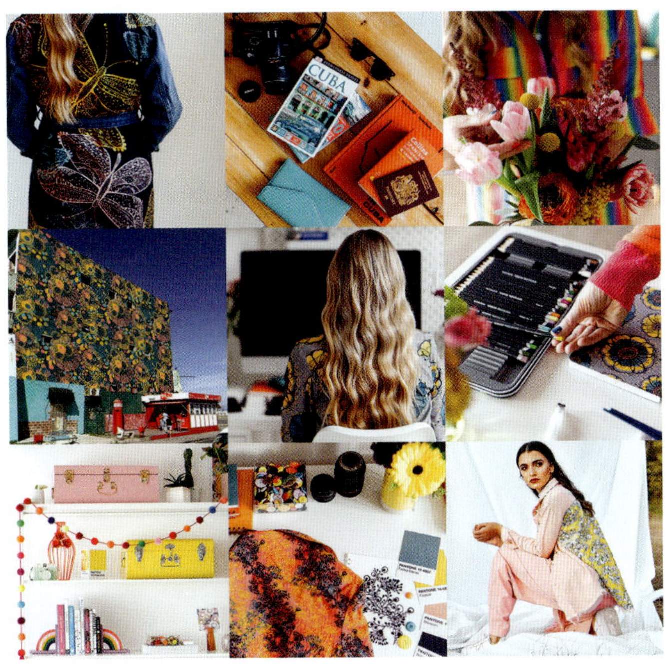

GRID OF NINE

A task I often set myself, and many of the creatives I coach, is to create a grid of nine images, as I find that this simple collage can give a real flavor for where you are. Feel free to print, cut out, and stick a physical version or create a digital version a bit like my example. You can also use image-editing apps on your phone to do this.

First, I tend to put an image of me in the center and then eight other images around that which I feel sum up my project and the destination I had in mind. I describe myself as a multidisciplinary creative, but these three titles really sum up my work best: art director, creative mentor, and pattern designer. I'm in a really good place with my work right now, so when I look at the images that show my current destination, I feel content.

However, if I felt uneasy about any of it, I could simply reshuffle the images and the result will show me where I need to nurture, scale back, or grow my creative offering. Or I could be bold, reevaluate, and try something completely new, resulting in a very different grid of nine.

Sometimes it only takes a simple task or a visual exercise to make us reflect on what we really want, and in turn what we don't want. This can also be a great exercise when pitching to work with someone and seeing if you fit well within a company's brand aesthetic. I would love to see you share your results with me on social media.

WHEN THINGS DON'T GO ACCORDING TO PLAN

Things do not always go to plan, and that's okay. We can change, refine, improve, and analyze, but most of all we need to be honest with ourselves about what we really want and see the meaning in a failure. As important as it is to celebrate, it's just as important to acknowledge failure and disappointment—things we don't need to view in a negative light. Lessons can be learned and if every day were always perfect, we wouldn't appreciate our success. The tough times make the good times taste that much sweeter. So many people go through many of the same failures and disappointments.

When a Great Idea Isn't Actually That Great

Knowing when to pull the plug on things, especially on something you thought was a great idea, can be hard. Years ago, my business partner Beth Kempton and I came up with an idea for a designer directory. It was a great concept and a platform where we would promote designers, particularly the students of our online courses.

We worked with some great third parties and invested time and money, but in the end found there were too many problems to make it a sustainable idea. The software we needed kept changing, there was too much competition, and it just wasn't viable economically.

So even though we had invested time and money, we knew we needed to pull the plug. It was better to do that early on, rather than drag it out and worry about admitting defeat. I think sometimes when something doesn't go to plan, we don't want to say, "Oh no, I made a mistake," but once we've admitted that we know that things will be okay. Try not to be hard on yourself; you can only predict so much and sometimes things happen that are out of your control.

I know it can be hard when someone tells you to look on the bright side of things, but there is a lot of truth in it. For every cloud there's a silver lining and for every X there's a Y. Try filling out your own Xs and Ys in the following list and see the good with the bad.

X let me down, but I know I can count on Y.
X was horrible, but Y was amazing for me.
X needs to end, but I might be able to work on Y.
X didn't work at all, but I did learn Y.
X doesn't look right, but I do like Y.

I always follow my dreams even if a plan hasn't gone well. When that happens, I go on to what might be the next best idea, or I go back and improve or adapt what I had envisioned. I just never give up on getting to my destination, and I don't want you to either.

Make things happen and have the courage to dream big.

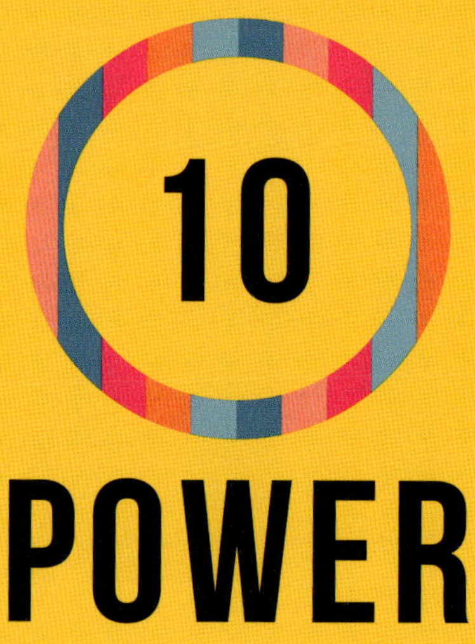

10 POWER

How do I know—and own—my power?

> "Everything you can imagine is real."
> —Pablo Picasso

I hope as you have navigated through this book you have been on a journey of self-discovery and that you truly recognize, or are at least beginning to recognize, the power of your creativity and self-worth. Throughout the stages of our lives and careers there will be times when we feel that our light isn't shining so brightly and other times when it feels supercharged. If we open up our mind and hearts and strive to go forward with authenticity and courage, then we can unlock the doors to many more opportunities and gain confidence in recognizing our full capabilities. Only then can we start to feel comfortable accepting what makes us special and what we can offer to the world.

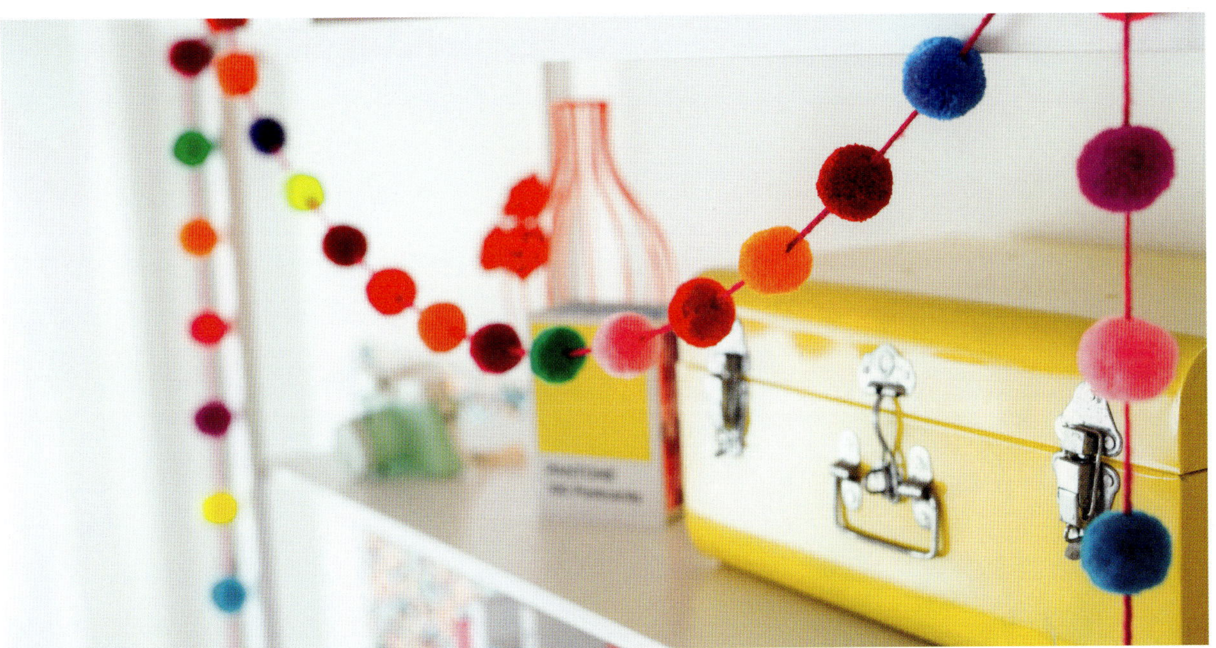

THOUGHTS TO PONDER ON POWER

An important topic (and usually an uncomfortable one for many) that I want to touch on is money. As creatives, we want to share our gift with the world, and though we might offer free work for goodwill or charity from time to time, remember that your art took you time and effort to master. It's vital to charge what your work is worth and not undercharge or undersell yourself, especially if you rely on your creative output as your sole income. If your painting hangs on someone's wall in a beautiful home, why should you be treated any differently to the paid builder that renovated the room? Plus, our creativity can go way beyond materialistic improvements. Our creations can hold so much power as they can remind people of their happiest or most important memory, soothe the senses, evoke moods and emotions, reflect personalities, and turn a house into a home.

Even when we're creating for more of a hobby, we can receive commissions to create for friends or family. In these instances, we can feel wrong charging for our work; after all, we do it because we love it. But if that commission is taking you away from your own work, work that provides income, then there should be no sense of guilt when charging for your time and skills. There's so much power in knowing that other people aren't doing you a favor by buying your art; you're providing your services and talent and have created something that they are going to cherish.

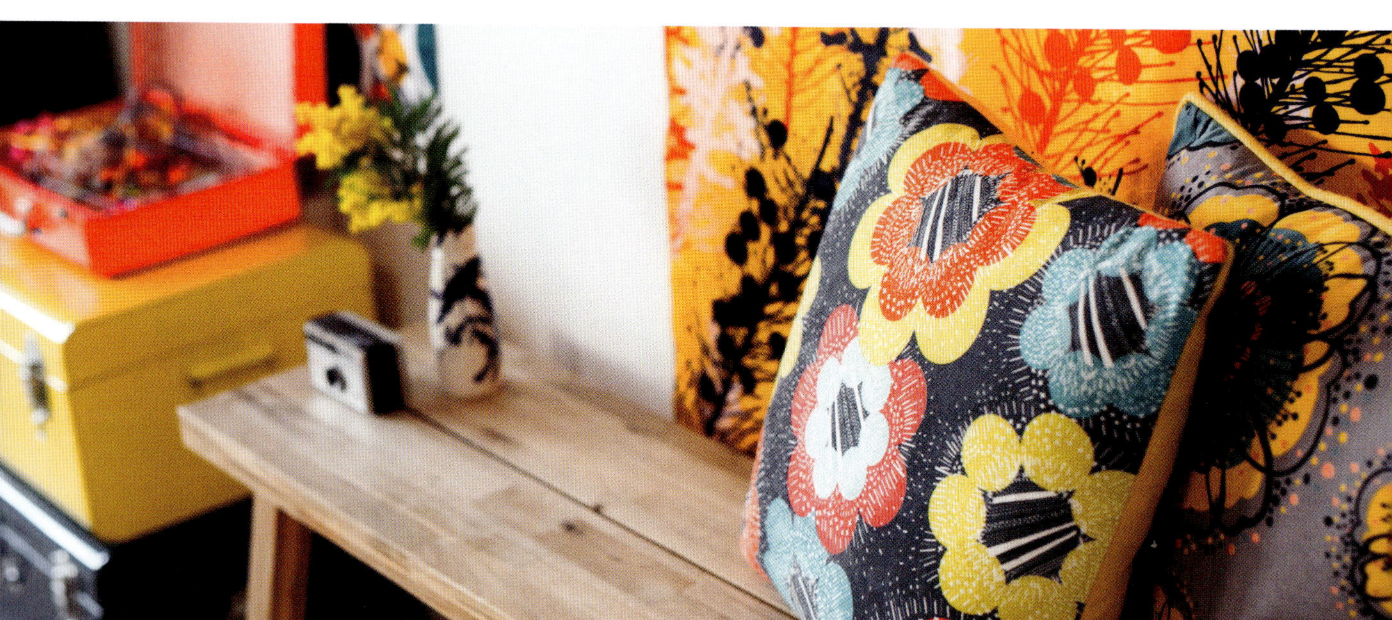

CREATIVE EXERCISES

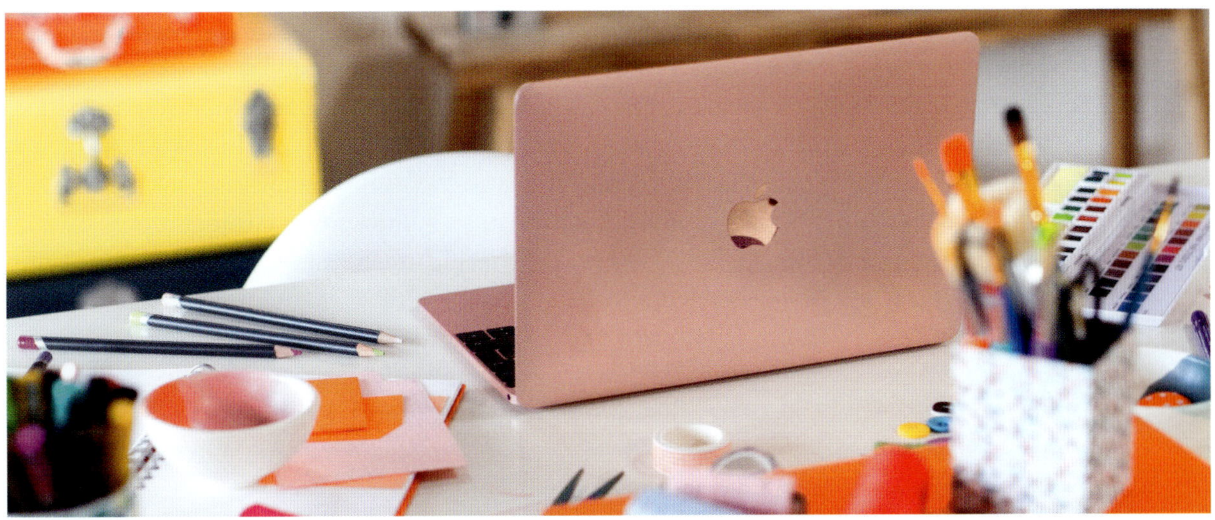

FIND POWER IN NEGOTIATION

Another important and yet uncomfortable topic I want to talk about is negotiating. I honestly used to break out in a sweat at the thought of asking for a pay raise, increasing my hourly rate, or requesting an advance or increased royalty. After many years in the industry, I now know that I can receive better—and more importantly, deserve better.

Often as creatives we are so flattered to receive paid work, because our job is often our true passion. When we land that dream client, we can freak out with imposter syndrome and then ultimately worry about asking for what we really deserve.

I've been doing this a long time and trust me when I say that the majority of the time there is wiggle room with fees when a company really wants to secure you working for them. If you feel you have landed a deal you deserve, you naturally work better as you feel more confident in your skills, which can deepen the faith and trust they have in you. When you are feeling the pressure, remind yourself that *they chose you* for the project, so keep being unapologetically you and own that.

SHARED EXPERIENCE

I recently advised one of my coaching clients, Kate Merritt, based in France, on this very matter when she had been offered a deal where she knew she deserved better compensation but felt very nervous responding, worried that they would think she was being brutal and unfriendly. I reminded Kate that you can still have a friendly manner while being firm and professional and asking for what you want. Initially she was so excited about the project, but after seeing the contract, her enthusiasm for the project dipped. If the financial aspect is impacting you so much so that it affects your excitement to work on something, then it's important to address that before it escalates. If you don't feel it's a fair deal and still decide to take on the work, subconsciously it can cause resentment and that is something that will show in your work. In this case, my client had been put on the spot in a video call, but she had the good sense to ask for more time to think about the offer. After we talked, Kate jotted down what her ideal offer would be and that is what she took to the negotiations. Even though behind the scenes she felt nervous, in the end she really owned her worth and had the courage to secure what she thoroughly deserved. The tips I provided Kate were:

- Avoid agreeing to anything face to face or straight away, especially when you feel put on the spot.
- Take some time to evaluate the offer.
- Write a pros and cons list.
- Jot down all the things that you really want from the offer.
- Envision your dream number or amount.

Here's a list of the kinds of things you can negotiate on and discuss:

- An advance against sales of royalties.
- A deposit for a commission (even if the job is for a friend).
- A percentage, daily rate, or ideal fee.
- Free samples and a wholesale rate for selling on your own platforms.
- A short statement of what you can bring to the table, such as "unique exclusive print from a designer with a strong identity signature style and with her own customer base and loyal audience".
- What you can offer your clients, such as a complimentary consultation, a preview of the design or art in process, openness to feedback, flexibility of design changes, or complimentary recolors.
- Complimentary work such as coordinating pieces or a printed and signed (maybe framed) copy of the original art.
- Copyright and ownership.
- Social media posts and promotion.

I find that most negotiations go the same way. If you ask for an increase and tell them a figure you had in mind, they will either meet you halfway or go slightly lower than you envisioned. Therefore, I advise that you always have your dream number in mind and even increase it slightly, as more often than not you'll come away with what you initially wanted. (Oops if my clients are reading this, please forgive me!) However, if a budget is limited and there isn't much wiggle room, then you can ask for things such as an advance, free samples, a shorter licensing term, or a more flexible and less exclusive contract. Sometimes we just need a bit of encouragement to recognize that we have so much power over what we want, and I hope this example does that for you.

It's within your power to lead a creative life that you love and *you* have the ability to change things. Every day is another chance to become a step closer to the thing you want. Remember that if you ever need to pause, it's okay; the plan can change, but the end goal doesn't have to.

Even with the many difficult bumps in the road that I've hit along the way, nothing seems impossible to me anymore and I truly believe this can be the case for anyone. Half the battle is recognizing your own worth, tuning out the negativity, and simply working hard. I hope in having shared my own stories and conversations throughout this book that you are able to recognize that reality for yourself as well.

ACKNOWLEDGE YOUR KNOWLEDGE

Right now I want you to own your skills and *acknowledge your knowledge*. Focus on your successes and celebrate them—jot them down, pin it on your wall, stick it on the fridge, pop it on your desktop. It's funny, you don't realize how much you've worked on or achieved until it is visually in front of you. I think you might just surprise yourself!

An example of this was when I grouped all the magazines I've been published in over the years for a photoshoot. I felt so blessed to have had my words, images, and designs put out there for the world to see.

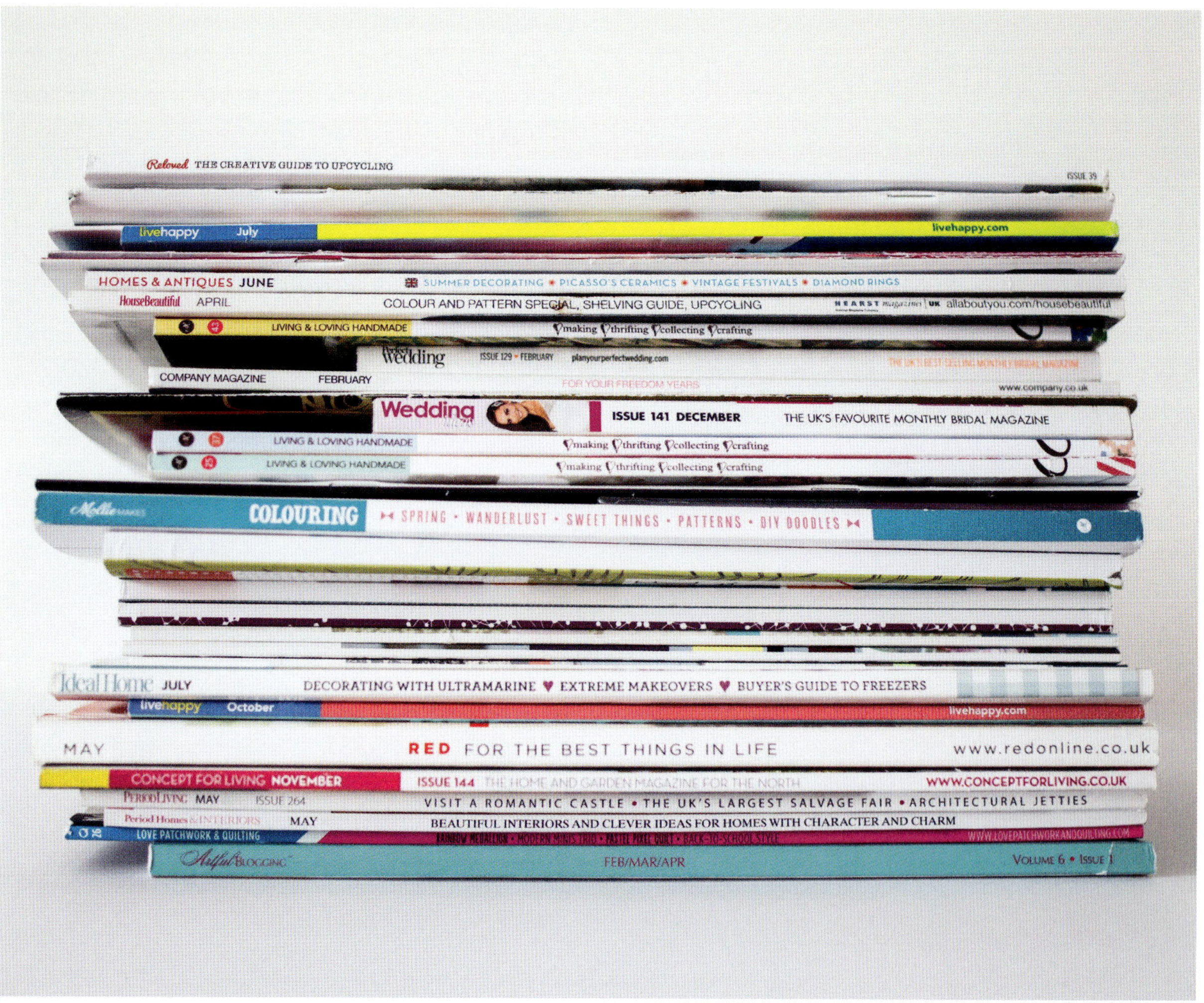

At times we can fail to recognize what it is that can give us our power. Without overthinking it, I'd like you to make a list of your top five personality traits and creative abilities.

Here are my personality traits as an example:

- I'm honest.
- I'm resourceful.
- I'm kind.
- I'm an empath.
- My energy helps motivate and inspire other creatives.

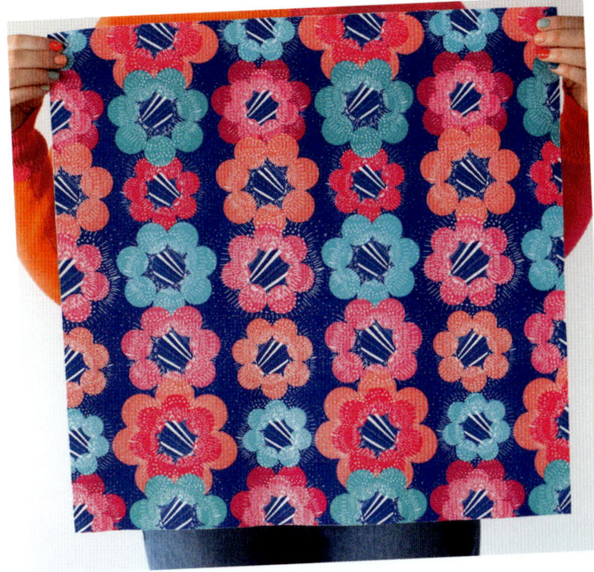

And my top creative abilities:

- I'm known as the pattern queen.
- I can draw with both my right and left hands.
- My work makes people smile and feel happy.
- My designs ooze color confidence.
- I have a strong, recognizable, signature creative style.

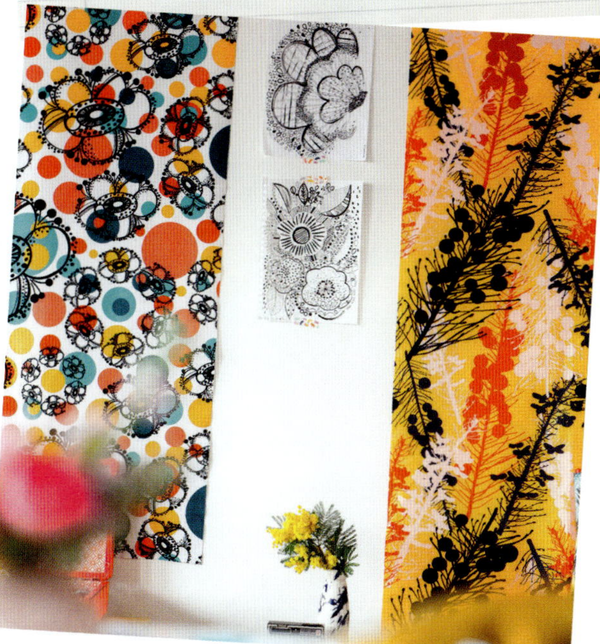

THE POWER OF PERSPECTIVE

Know that you can create anything
that you put your mind to.

At times during my career, I have felt uncomfortable as my name slowly became a trademark. I'd have to say things like "the Rachael Taylor collection" out loud a lot and it would feel strange and almost arrogant. At times I would feel imposter syndrome when reaching out to clients. In those early days using my personal name could have potentially held me back from having the confidence to put myself out there. I'm a lot more used to it now, but that acceptance only came from shifting my perspective. For instance, it helped to think of it more like, what if this were my best friend's business, or a family member's business? Wouldn't I use the best language when describing it? Wouldn't I be so passionate and energetic about it and helping support and promote it? Wouldn't I be helping get the idea out there, shining it in its best light, and making sure it really succeeds?

I encourage you to try this for yourself if you feel that the personal nature of your creativity is holding you back. Once you think of it another way it can be easier to get more comfortable if you are struggling with promoting something so close to you.

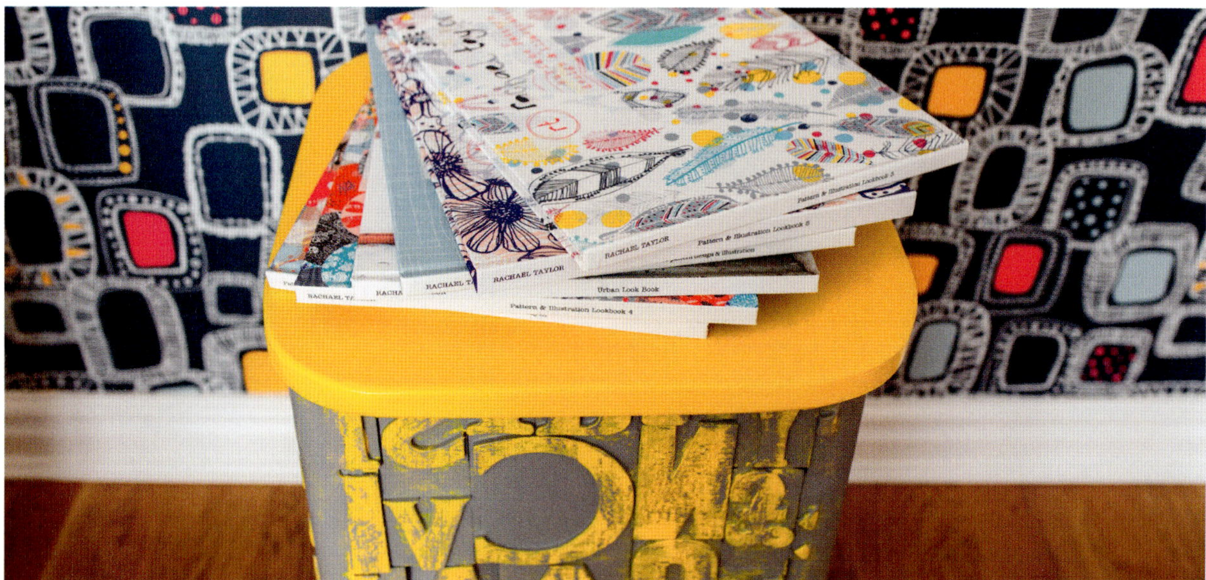

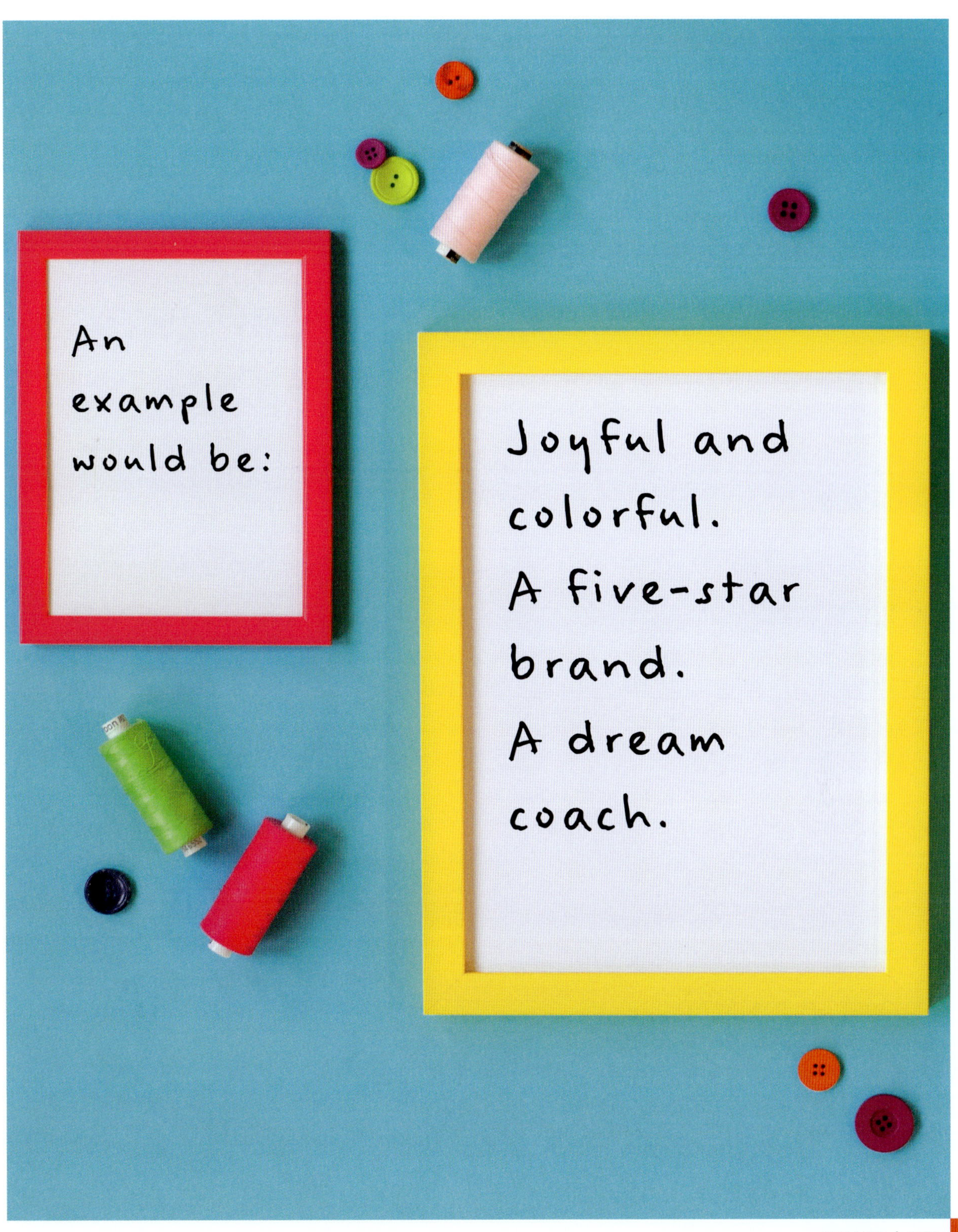
An
example
would be:
Joyful and
colorful.
A five-star
brand.
A dream
coach.

MANIFESTATION

It may sound cheesy, but if you believe it, you can achieve it. There is so much power in trying to manifest what we want, and it really has worked for me a number of times over the years (we touched on this in chapter 4, CLARITY, where I encouraged you to say your dreams out loud). Ways in which we can help manifest what we want:

- Say it out loud—to a friend, family member, or colleague.
- Write it down—save it or pin it somewhere you'll always see it.
- Change your social bio to reflect whatever it is (one year I wanted to be a travel writer, so I put that in my bio).
- Reach out and network—send friendly but professional emails or direct messages to people who are already doing what you want to do, and maybe they can help you.
- Fake it until you make it. If you want to see your creative work on buildings someday, learn how to create a mock-up, do it for yourself, and get it out there.

Are there other ways you could manifest what you want to do with your creativity? Jot them down and find the time to make them happen.

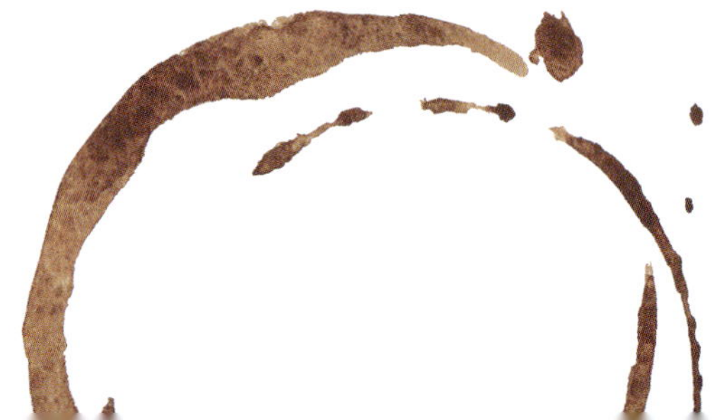

SHARE YOUR MAGIC

There are times as creatives when we are ready to put our idea out there, but we find something is stopping us. Whether it's doubt (will anyone actually want to buy what we've created?) or concern that it won't actually be lucrative, or even that we haven't made something unique enough, there can be so many obstacles. It's all about taking that leap, adding a dash of bravery, and having the confidence to put yourself out there. Know that the world deserves to see your creative magic.

Stay in love with what you have created. Be so happy and positive talking about it. If you don't believe in your work, how do you expect others to believe in it and get behind it? It's so important that your passion really shines through in everything that you do. I use the phrase "Patterns to Make You Happy" for my studio brand, as it's crucial that my design audience can absorb that feel-good energy in all of my creations.

If it helps to think of it in a different way, just remind yourself that one day your creation could mean a lot to someone. There will be people in the world who *want* your product or to hire your services because they believe in what you are doing. So if you don't put the message out there, you're missing that feeling of having provided something truly special to someone.

Take a moment to think about what you would ideally love to happen once you've shared your creation or reached your goal. What would people say? How would they react? How will it have helped them? What would be your dream review? Write it down or envision it happening. This comes back to manifesting what we want—putting it out into the world and believing it will happen. Be brave, have courage, put yourself out there, and embrace the unknown and all those opportunities with open arms. You won't regret it!

When you make magic
the world deserves to see it.

AFTERWORD

I want to thank you for showing up and for your bravery, time, energy, and commitment. This book is always here for you to read again and again, to dip in and out of when you need a guide or a sense of clarity. Feel free to keep it on your favorite coffee table, workstation, or at your desk and see it as a comfort to steer you through both exciting and turbulent times.

Though we may have reached the end of this book, your exciting journey will continue, and you must always remember to celebrate *you* and your magical gift . . . your creativity.

Celebrate your past self, whose previous creative endeavors (good or bad) have made you the person you are today.

Celebrate your present self, you who are reading my words right now and chose to power up your creativity and invest in yourself.

Celebrate the future and unknown you, the wheels you have put in motion, and opportunities that might just surprise you one day.

I'm forever working on my own creative adventures and often provide free resources such as webinars, online classes, competitions, scholarships, and podcasts, so please do keep in touch via makeitindesign.com and rachaeltaylordesigns.com and via Instagram: @makeitindesign and @rachaeltstudio. There is also a dedicated Facebook group full of free resources and a supportive community to accompany this book: facebook.com/groups/powerupyourcreativity. I would love for you share your experience using #powerupyourcreativity and show you reading your book, and where you are reading it. I will share and cherish your progress and wins, and I will always be your biggest cheerleader. I want you to reach your full potential and live the creative life you have always imagined.

I believe in you, and now it's time for you to believe in you too.

Rachael xo

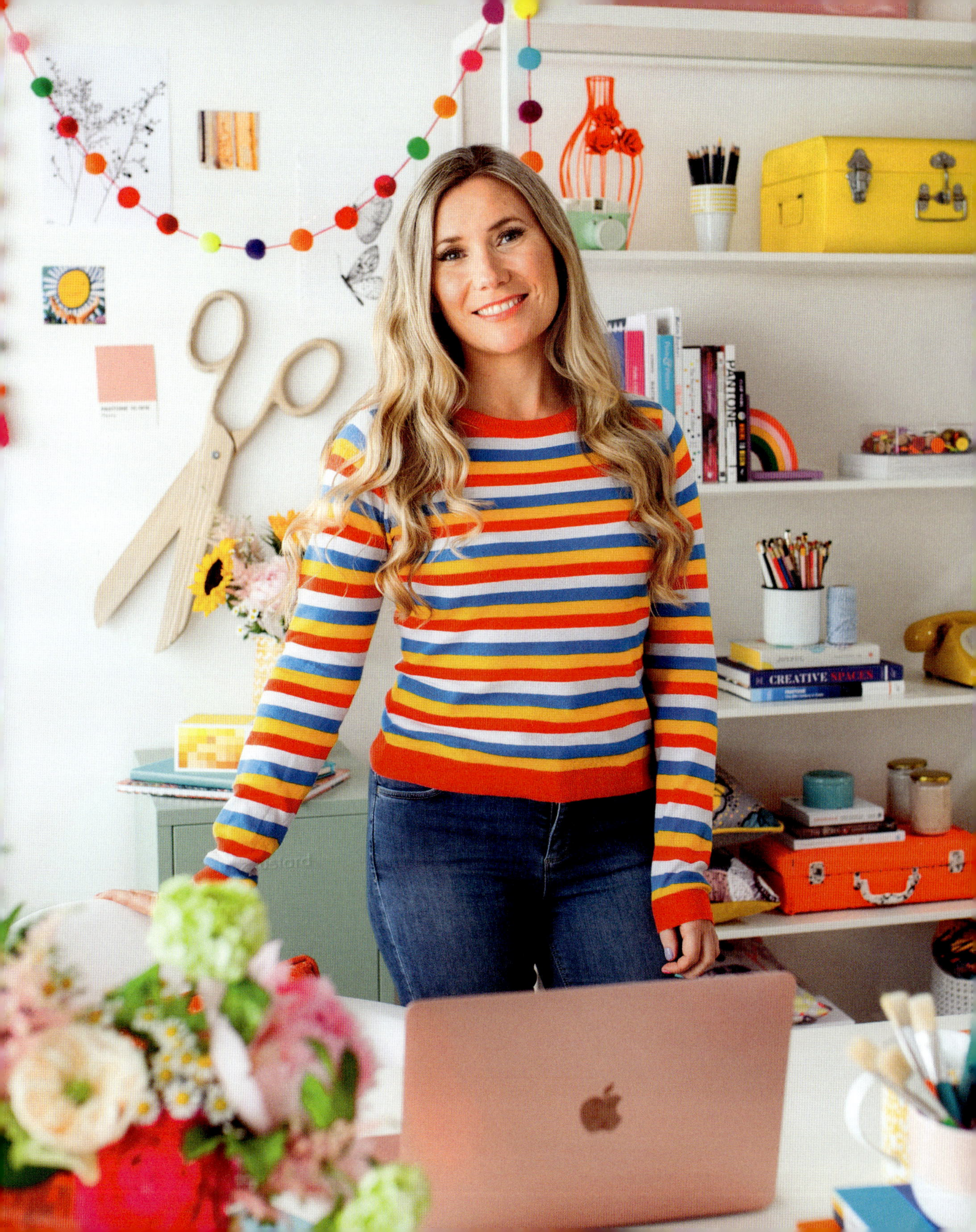
PANTONE
CREATIVE SPACES

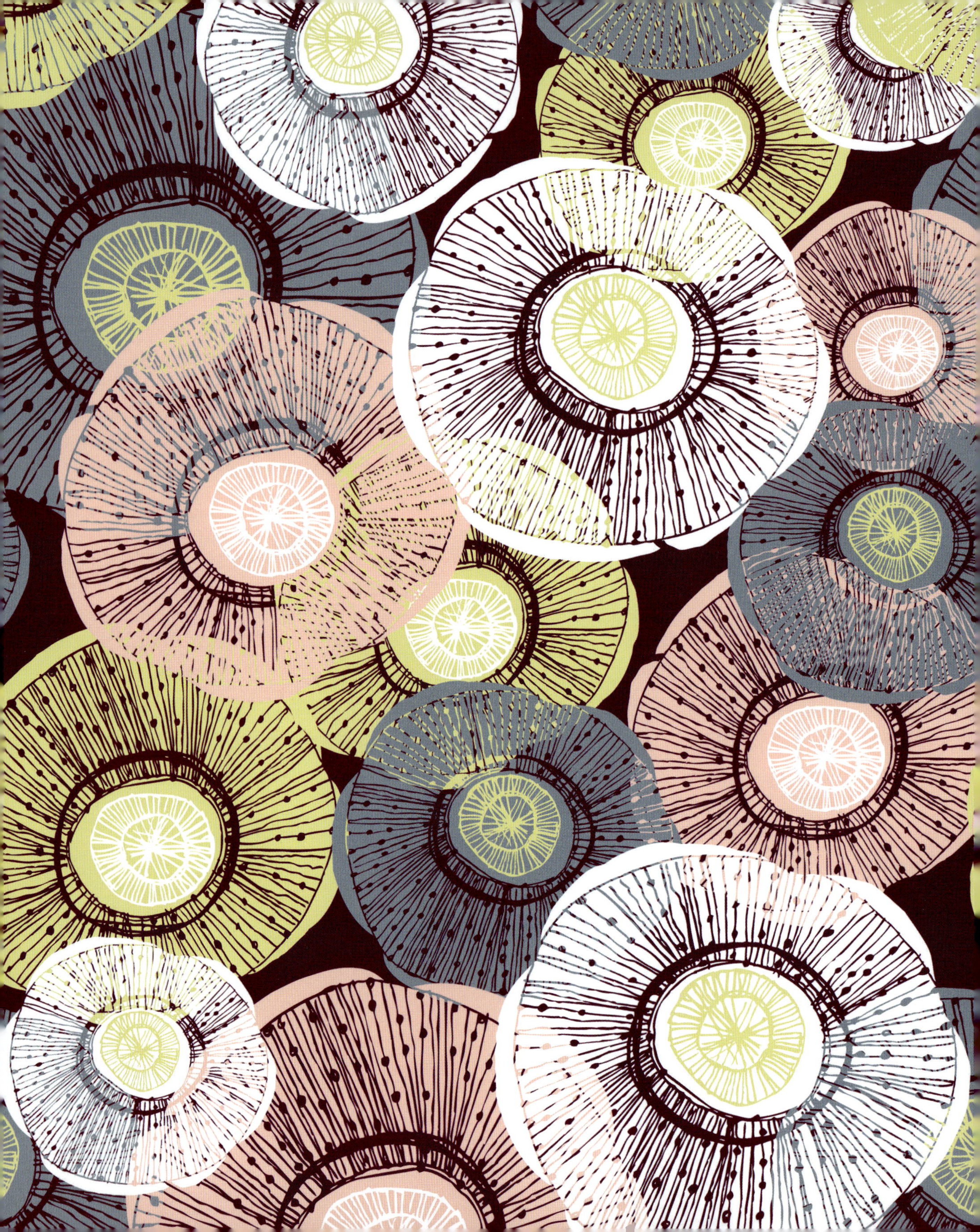

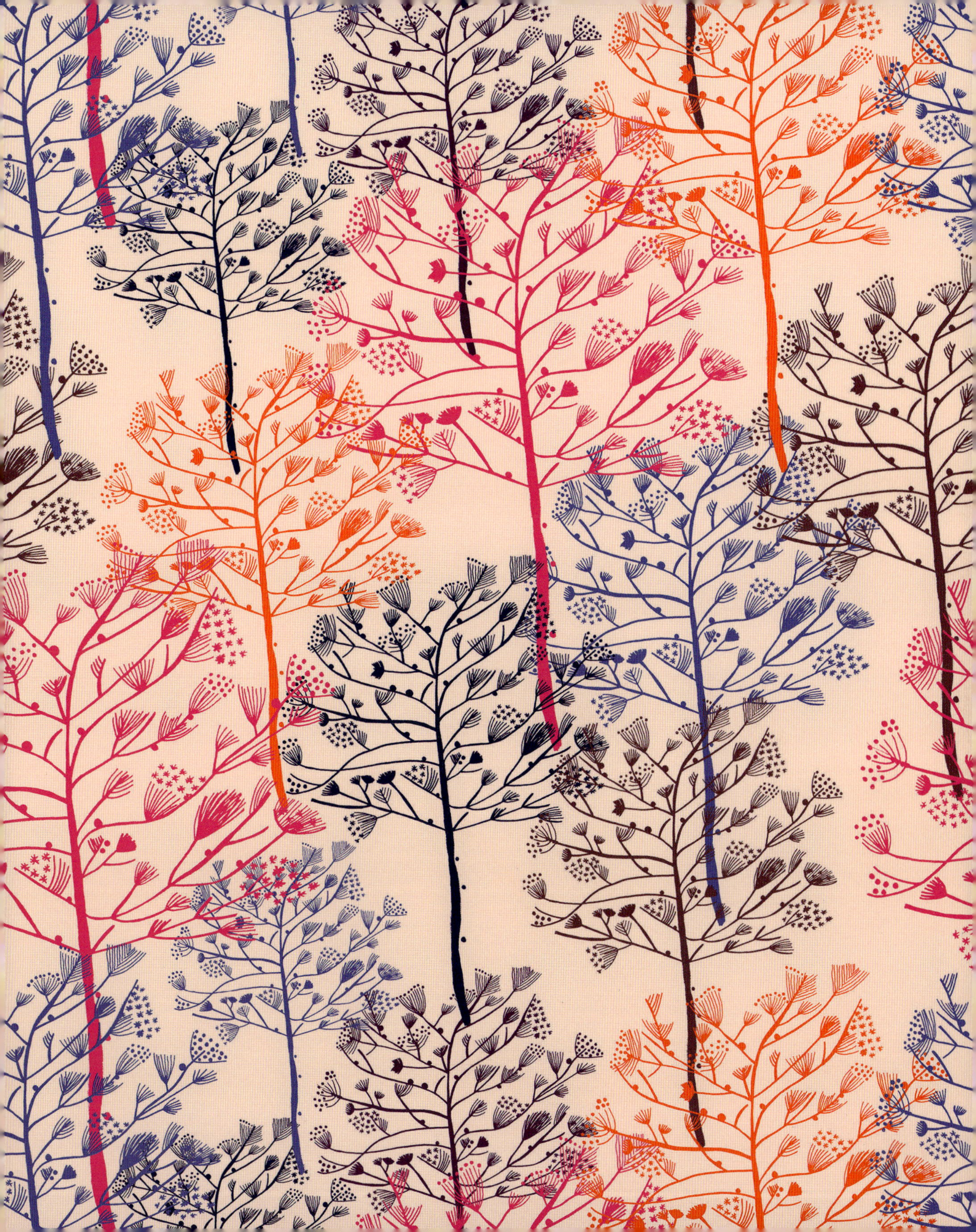

RESOURCES

I have collated a broad list of resources that I thought would be useful for you, my lovely reader. Please note that this is condensed, as I could have filled a lot more pages with how much brilliant support and talent there is out there.

AGENTS AND STUDIOS

Advocate Art
www.advocate-art.com

Cinnamon Joe Studio
www.cinnamonjoestudio.com

Lilla Rogers
www.lillarogers.com

Lemon Ribbon
www.lemonribbon.com

Pink Light Studio
www.pinklightstudio.com

Paper and Cloth
www.paperandcloth.co.uk

AMAZING CREATIVES AND BRANDS

Alison Cole
www.allisoncoleillustration.com

Annabel Tempest
www.annabeltempest.com

Donna Wilson
www.donnawilson.com

Coral and Moss
www.coralandmoss.co

Cece & Bear
www.instagram.com/cece.and.bear

Charlotte Jade
www.charlotte-jade.co.uk

Elizabeth Olwen
www.elizabetholwen.com

Emily Coxhead
www.emilycoxhead.com

Dashwood Studio
www.dashwoodstudio.com

Davinder Madaher
www.davindermadaher.com

Do What You Love
www.dowhatyouloveforlife.com

Faye Brown
www.fayebrown.co.uk

Fiona Humberstone
www.thebrand-stylist.com

Fizah Malik
www.fizahmalikdesigns.com

Gemma Longworth
www.instagram.com/gemma_longworth_diy

James Martin
www.themadebyjames.com

Jay Blades
www.jayblades.co.uk

Janine Burrows
www.janineburrows.co.uk

Jess Williams
www.jesswilliams.co.uk

Louise Tiler
www.louisetiler.com

Little Tweet Art
www.instagram.com/littletweetart

Kelle Boyd
www.annkelle.com

Kieron Lewis
www.kieronlewis.com

Magic and Monroe
www.magicandmonroe.co.uk

Maria Montiel
www.mariamontielstudio.com

Marianne Shillingford
www.instagram.com/m_shillingford

Mark Knowles
www.makcreativeuk.co.uk

Mister Fred
www.misterfred.org

Nutmeg Studio
www.nutmegwallartstickers.co.uk

Reloved Upholstery
www.relovedupholstery.co.uk

Rachel Westhead
www.rachelwestheaddesigns.co.uk

Rob Ryan
www.robryanstudio.com

Sophie Robinson
www.sophierobinson.co.uk

Sophie Tea
www.sophieteaart.com

sundownmoonup
www.instagram.com/sundownmoonup_

Terry Runyan
www.terryrunyan.com

Zeena Shah
www.instagram.com/heartzeena

Zoe Ingram
www.zoeingram.com

ART MATERIALS

Derwent
www.derwentart.com

Pink Pig
www.the-pink-pig.co.uk

Wacom
www.wacom.com

BUSINESS

Creative Coaching Sessions with Rachael Taylor
www.rachaeltaylordesigns.com/coaching

Holly & Co
www.holly.co

The Design Trust
www.thedesigntrust.co.uk

The Ladder Club
www.pgbuzz.net/the-ladder-club

COLOR

Adobe Color
color.adobe.com

Coolors
www.coolors.co

Designspiration
www.designspiration.com

Pantone
www.pantone.com

COPYRIGHT AND INTELLECTUAL PROPERTY

Alliance for Intellectual Property
www.allianceforip.co.uk

Anti-Copying in Design (ACID)
www.acid.uk.com

McDaniels Law
www.mcdanielslaw.com

World Intellectual Property Organization
www.wipo.int

DESIGN SOFTWARE

Adobe
www.adobe.com

Affinity Designer
www.affinity.serif.com

Canva
www.canva.com

Procreate
www.procreate.art

INSPIRATION

Creative Boom
www.creativeboom.com

Creative Bloq
www.creativebloq.com

Creative Review
www.creativereview.co.uk

Design Clever
www.designclever.co.uk

Design Week
www.designweek.co.uk

Design Taxi
www.designtaxi.com

Dribbble
www.dribbble.com

Google Design
www.design.google

Httpster
www.httpster.net

Inspiration Grid
www.theinspirationgrid.com

It's Nice That
www.itsnicethat.com

Made By Folk
www.madebyfolk.com

Pattern Curator
www.patterncurator.com

Print and Pattern
www.printpattern.blogspot.com

Shillington Design Blog
www.shillingtoneducation.com/blog

The Dieline
www.thedieline.com

MAGAZINES

91 Magazine
www.91magazine.co.uk

Breathe
www.breathemagazine.com

Computer Arts
www.creativebloq.com/computer-arts-magazine

Creative Pro
www.creativepro.com

Creative Review
www.creativereview.co.uk

Design Week
www.designweek.co.uk

Elle Decor
www.elledecor.com

Eye
www.eyemagazine.com

Flow
www.flowmagazine.com

Frankie
www.frankie.com.au

Mindsparkle Mag
www.mindsparklemag.com

Mollie Makes
www.gathered.how/magazines-mollie-makes

Progressive Greetings
www.pgbuzz.net/pgmagazine/progressive-greetings-worldwide

Reclaim
www.reclaimmagazine.uk

Smashing Magazine
www.smashingmagazine.com

Uppercase
www.uppercasemagazine.com

Wallpaper
www.wallpaper.com

What Women Create and Where Women Create
www.womencreate.com

MEMBERS' CLUBS

AOI
www.theaoi.com

The Make It In Design Live Hub
www.makeitindesign.com/livehub

MY ONLINE COURSES

Make It In Design
www.makeitindesign.com

NETWORKING

LinkedIn
www.linkedin.com

Hunter
www.hunter.io

PHOTOGRAPHY AND STYLING

Capture By Lucy
www.capturebylucy.com

Colorplan paper
www.gfsmith.com

Fairclough Studios
www.faircloughstudios.co.uk

Holly Booth Studio
www.hollybooth.com

The Struths Photography
www.struthphotography.com

Teresa C Photography
www.teresac.co.uk

PODCASTS

Conversations of Inspiration Podcast
www.holly.co/podcast

Create!
www.createmagazine.com/podcast

Creative Boom Podcast
www.creativeboom.com/podcast

Creative Pep Talk
www.creativepeptalk.com

Creative Rebels
www.instagram.com/rebelscreate

Crafty Ass Female
www.craftyassfemale.com

Design Matters
www.designmattersmedia.com

Happy Place Podcast
www.happyplaceofficial.co.uk

Hashtag Authentic
www.meandorla.co.uk/the-podcast

Overshare: Honest Conversations with Creatives
https://overshare.simplecast.com

The Creativity Campus
www.instagram.com/the_creativity_campus_official

The Great Indoors
www.madaboutthehouse.com/podcast

The Make it in Design Podcast
www.makeitindesign.com/the-make-it-in-design-podcast

Thriving Women Artists
www.thrivingwomenartists.com

Windowsill Chats
www.tantaustudio.com/podcast

PRINTING AND MANUFACTURING

Countryside Art
www.countrysideart.co.uk

Century Studios
www.centurystudios.co.uk

Maake
www.maake.com

R A Smart
www.rasmart.co.uk

Spoonflower
www.spoonflower.com

Contrado
www.contrado.co.uk

SHARED EXPERIENCE CONTRIBUTORS

Catherine Worsley
www.northernlightscreative.co.uk

Kate Merritt
www.katemerritt.com

Georgina Van Hasselt
www.whistlingthorn.co.uk

Lindsay Elissa Coils
www.slinkeee.com

Monica Escobar
www.italillywhite.wordpress.com

Paige Stevens Holsapple
www.paigeholsapple.carbonmade.com

Sarah Chaudry
www.sarahalice.art

Vibeke Larsen
www.poppydesign.no

SOCIAL MEDIA APPS

Adobe Premiere Rush
www.adobe.com

Behance
www.behance.net

Darkroom
www.darkroom.co

Discord
www.discord.com

Facebook
www.facebook.com

Filmm
www.filmm.co

Hootsuite
www.hootsuite.com

Infltr
www.infltr.com

Instagram
www.instagram.com

Later
www.later.com

Pinterest
www.pinterest.com

Pixlr
www.pixlr.com

Planoly
www.planoly.com

Template
www.templateapp.co

Twitter
www.twitter.com

VSCO
www.vsco.co

THOUGHT-PROVOKING WRITERS

Atticus
www.instagram.com/atticuspoetry

Beth Kempton
www.bethkempton.com

Bianca Sparacino
www.instagram.com/rainbowsalt

Cleo Wade
www.instagram.com/cleowade

Matt Haig
www.matthaig.com

Morgan Harper Nichols
www.morganharpernichols.com

Rupi Kaur
www.rupikaur.com

Yung Pueblo
www.instagram.com/yung_pueblo

TRADE SHOWS

Autumn Fair
www.autumnfair.com

Blue Print
www.blue-print-online.com

British Craft Trade Fair
www.bctf.co.uk

Creativa
www.messe-creativa.de

Decor + Design Melbourne
www.decordesignshow.com.au

Decorex
www.decorex.com

Design Shanghai
www.designshanghai.com

Design Show Australia
www.designshow.com.au

Fabric & Accessories Trade show
www.fnashow.in

Grand Designs Live
www.granddesignslive.com

Home & Gift
www.homeandgift.co.uk

Ideal Home Show
www.idealhomeshow.co.uk

Licensing Expo
www.licensingexpo.com

London Stationery Show
www.stationeryshowlondon.co.uk

Maison Objet
www.maison-objet.com

Premiere Vision
https://paris.premierevision.com/en

Printsource New York
www.printsourcenewyork.com

Progressive Greetings
www.progressivegreetingslive.com

Salone del Mobile
www.salonemilano.it

Spring Fair
www.springfair.com

Surtex
www.surtex.com

The Design Show Egypt
www.thedesign-show.com

The London Print Design Fair
www.thelondonprintdesignfair.co.uk

The Warsaw Home
www.warsawhome.eu

The Toronto Home Shows
www.torontohomeshows.com

Top Drawer
www.topdrawer.co.uk

TRENDS

Porter & Brawn
https://porterandbrawn.com

WGSN
www.wgsn.com

Trend Bible
www.trendbible.com

Trend Book
www.trendesignbook.com

The Better Trends Company
www.thebettertrendscompany.com

WEBSITE DESIGN AND BUILDING

123 Reg
www.123-reg.co.uk

ALSO
www.also-online.com

Bluehost
www.bluehost.com

Chris Murray
www.chrismurray.website

Fasthosts
www.fasthosts.co.uk

Ionos
www.ionos.co.uk

Shopify
www.shopify.co.uk

Site 123
https://www.site123.com

Squarespace
www.squarespace.com

We Are Branch
www.wearebranch.com

Webador
www.webador.co.uk

Wix
www.wix.com

Woocommerce
www.woocommerce.com

Wordpress
www.wordpress.com

Vitalized
www.vitalized.co.uk

ACKNOWLEDGMENTS

The idea of my very own creative book has been bouncing around for quite a while and I've always known that at the right time it will happen. I'm truly glad I waited, and I honestly feel that you are receiving a much better version of me and the right book now.

I owe much gratitude to every single person who has encouraged me creatively throughout my life. Those that have cheered me on and helped me through many of the mediums I have explored, to now my specialty of design. Sadly, even to this day, so many people are discouraged from taking a creative path as they are told to "stop dreaming" or "get a real job." Luckily for me, my cheerleaders outweighed the naysayers and I want to thank myself here for being stubborn enough and driven enough to prove people wrong and going ahead and doing it anyway. I hope this book encourages you to follow your own brave creative heart.

Ever since I was little, I have always been a person who is constantly bursting with ideas and looking for new avenues through which I can express myself. As a child, I loved drama, dance, and art, and it was apparent from an early age that I loved to create and that I did not like to sit still. Back then, I shied away from routine, and even as an adult, I still describe myself as a genuine fidget. I love being surrounded by creative clutter. My creativity as a child led me to pursue an artistic path in high school, and along with a truly inspirational teacher, Ali—aka Miss McWatt, who saw the potential in me—my creativity saw me through some extreme episodes of bullying at crucial times in my education. I even had to change schools. Her faith in me and tireless support helped nurture my talent and bring my confidence and grades back up, and I left high school feeling recharged and ready to show the world what I was made of. Looking back, I do try to carry the lessons and encouragement she showed me into my own business ethics and teachings for Make It In Design, an online design school that I cofounded. My education platform is really all about showing people that they can create—that they can be successful, regardless of what they've been through. Yes, that means you too!

A huge thank-you goes to my wonderful team over at Make It In Design, past and present, with whom I have just celebrated over a decade in business: in particular Beth Kempton, Paul Kempton, Kelly Crossley, Vic Dickenson, and Charlotte Clayton, along with our freelance support and many guest experts and collaborators. They are the most wonderful team anyone could wish for and each one of them plays a huge part in creating our magic.

I would especially like to highlight my business partner, Beth Kempton, who's been an inspirational figure in my life since the day we met. She has helped me really believe in myself and fearlessly go after what I want. She made me recognize that ongoing growth and learning is so important and that it's okay to live and work outside the status quo. In fact, I owe her another huge thanks as she kindly gifted me her Book Proposal Masterclass, and her brilliant advice and structured system played a huge part in me taking my book idea seriously.

The next spotlight goes to Kelly Crossley, who works for both Make It In Design and the Rachael Taylor Design Studio. She continues to astonish me with her multidisciplinary talents, efficiency, kindness, dedication, hard work, and organized approach. Without her support and calming influence, I definitely would have been very overwhelmed writing this book. From reading my messy early drafts to encouraging my honest writing style. She also worked so brilliantly in assisting me with my creative vision, design layouts, and ideas and has been truly instrumental to all aspects of this book.

I would also like to show gratitude to my international art agent, Lilla Rogers, and her lovely supportive team for landing me some really cool jobs over the years. I'm always so appreciative of their relaxed approach and flexibility with me.

Another big thank-you goes to the makeitindesign.com and rachaeltaylordesigns.com community. To this day I'm in awe of your dedication and achievements, but what I love most is seeing how supportive and encouraging you are with one another. That's how creative communities should be! Our online community has gotten me through some tricky times too. I'm forever influenced, enriched, inspired, and motivated by all the brilliant individuals and wonderful cultures that we celebrate. My life is truly better for you being a part of it, and I feel so honored to have been your mentor and tutor for many years.

To my clients past and present and industry peers, thank you for believing in me, hiring me, and collaborating with me. You have shaped me into the diverse designer, mentor and person I am today.

I owe lots of gratitude to the lovely team at Quarto, from my kind, trusting, and skilled editor Joy Aquilino for allowing my authentic voice to come through, to Winnie Danenbarger, the Senior Vice President and publishing director, for having faith in me. To Regina Grenier, for her brilliant art direction that really streamlined the process and clarified my vision for this book. To Anne Landa for her epic support and encouragement and all of the Quarto marketing team who have all played such important roles for turning my dream into a reality.

I want to give a shout to Holly Booth and Peter Salter at Holly Booth Studio for their brilliant attention to detail and for really listening to my creative vision when capturing the majority of the imagery for this book.

I'd also like to thank Kate Forrest for her great support and creativity over the years helping me feel more confident each time I'm made up for camera.

A thank-you also goes to my Cuban-based photography and style squad, David Diaz, Carolina Lopez Tejero, and Suny González Lozano, for all the wonderful on-location images over the years and the creative growth, laughter, and Spanish lessons.

Another big acknowledgment has to be to my mum. Not only is she my biggest supporter but she could also shake the world with her resiliency, bravery, and strength. Her approach to living life to the fullest is a beautiful example to many. No matter what absurd idea I have, or when I'm running a million miles an hour on a project or have even fell in a big slump from exhaustion, she is the person who has my back. She never doubts me for a single second, encourages me but never pushes me, and has always given me freedom to just figure out who I am. I'm forever grateful for her style of parenting and being my inspiration and my rock. I would also like to thank all my close family members, in particular my auntie Paula and stepdad John for their ongoing love and support. They are there cheering me on no matter what.

To my most beautiful creation to date, my son Blayke: Thank you for showing me what true happiness is, making me feel complete, and never failing to make me smile every day. I hope that when you are old enough to understand this book it encourages you to continue with your own creative path. Keep bursting with those brilliant ideas of yours and you will forever provide sunshine on a rainy day to many.

A dedication goes to my gorgeous and kind Roo, thanks for driving me to my photoshoots and hunting down the best emergency props! You managed to keep me chilled out during this book-writing process. You make every day feel like an amazing adventure and have been an unexpected and wonderful gift. My life is all the better for loving you, thank you for embracing my quirks and always supporting me without judgement.

Thank you to many of my dear friends, from my loyal school friends to my lovely university friends especially Carrie, Beckie, Jen, Lisa, Steph, Liz, Gemma, Rach, Nicky, and my fab fellow creatives Vic, Libby, and Louise, who all became like sisters. To my newer friends, travel buddies, and my Cuba family for embracing my imperfect self. In particular I'm so grateful for Michel's bright light, amazing support, spiritual wisdom, and yoga encouragement, and to all who have really shown up during turbulent times and have been a bright beacon.

A shout-out also goes to Anne Gilbertston for her wonderful acupuncture treatments that have become such a necessity for my mental health and creative output.

Also, thank you to my right hand—the only one I type with. Despite being ambidextrous with almost everything, somehow, I rely on my right hand to type. We got there! Aches, cramped fingers, and all!

I also want to say I'm very grateful for my life. You see, just over twenty-four years ago my life was saved by a stranger—well, a guardian angel, really. I've never ever met that person and know nothing about them other than they were walking their dog. But without them acting so swiftly and the medics keeping me alive, I wouldn't be here writing this. I'm most grateful for being given a second chance at life, as I was told it's a miracle that I even survived. Perhaps a little bit deep for an acknowledgments page, but hey, I think we all take life for granted at times and I'm so grateful for the gift that it is. People often say I'm different or they haven't met anyone like me before. I think it's mostly said in a good way, I hope, and if not, I'm okay with not being everyone's cup of tea! But that experience made me who I am today, and I really do try to live life to the fullest. For example, I decided to write a book while undergoing dyslexia assessments. I hope overcoming my struggles can give you the courage to know you can overcome yours.

These past few years have probably been the most transformational years both personally and professionally. I feel like I've been growing and shedding my cocoon for quite some time, and I'm now able to truly spread my beautiful butterfly wings.

Last but not least, I want to thank you, my lovely audience, for showing up and reading my words and committing to powering up your creativity. I can't wait to watch you flourish.

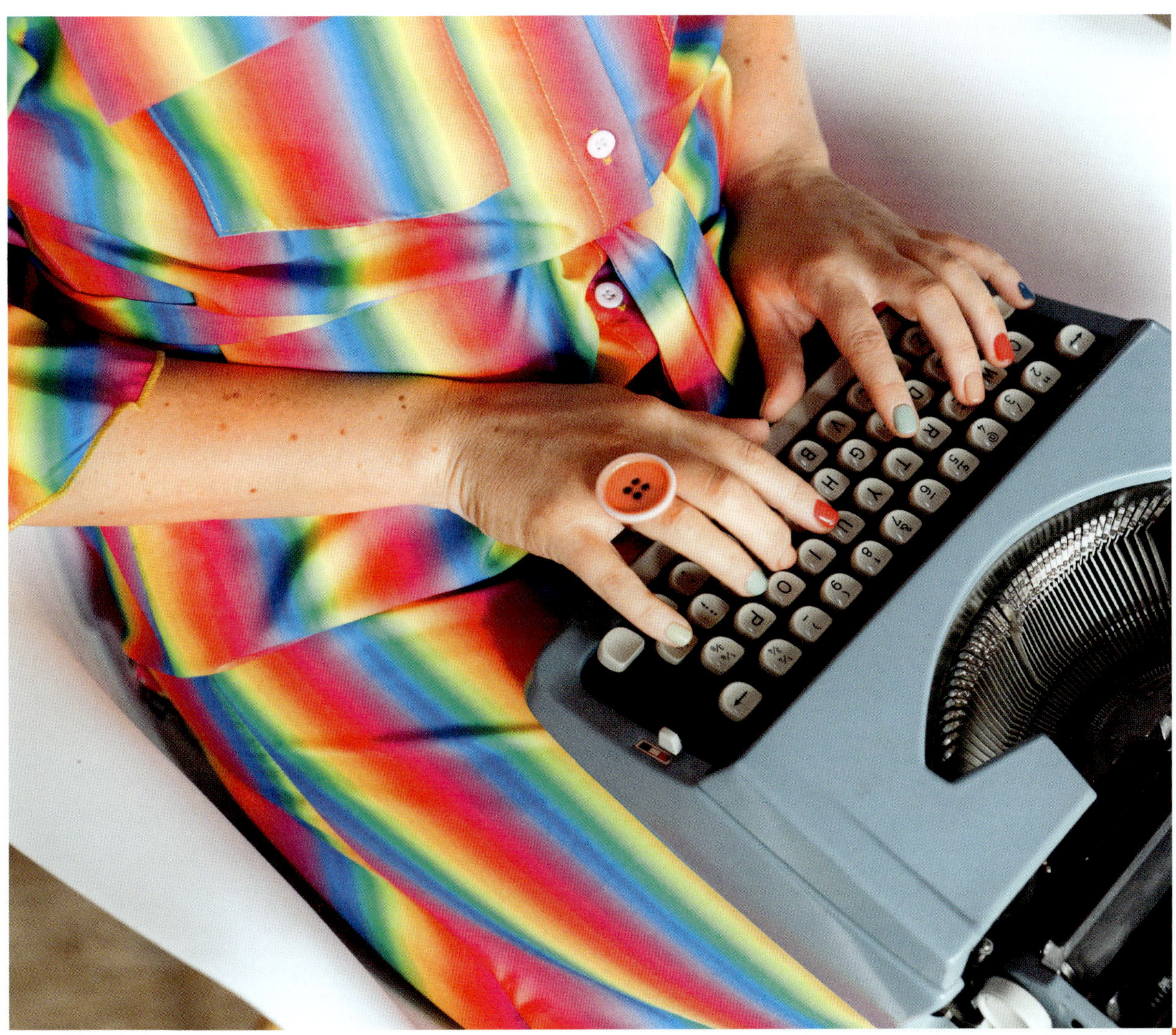

ABOUT THE AUTHOR

Rachael Taylor is an award-winning art director, creative mentor, and print and pattern designer. She is most known for her quirky style, daring use of color, and unique innovation. She regularly takes on design commissions for various companies and has created prints and patterns for almost every area in the marketplace. She is also a trademarked brand with a number of licensed products worldwide.

She is a much-loved coach and is often told that her teaching style is infectious, friendly, honest, informative, and motivational. Rachael approaches her students and clients with a sense of relatability and her services are often described as "talking to an old friend who just has the answers."

As cofounder of Make It In Design, Rachael has developed a groundbreaking educational online platform and taught more than 25,000 students across 100 countries.

Rachael is regularly featured in the media, from biographic pieces to her own articles sharing design advice. Highlights include *A House Beautiful Home Business, ITV, Channel 4, BBC, Print and Pattern, Red, Where Women Create, Ideal Home, Mollie Makes, and Homestyle*, to name a few. She is also a member of the UK government's Anti-Copying in Design Sector Council.

You will also find Rachael regularly speaking at design industry events and she adores creative writing. You can connect with Rachael at:

Instagram: @rachaeltaylor_ @rachaeltstudio @makeitindesign
Twitter: @rachael_taylor_ @RachaelTStudio @makeitindesign.com
Facebook: /rachaeltaylordesigns and /makeitindesign
Facebook group: facebook.com/groups/powerupyourcreativity
Web: rachaeltaylordesigns.com and makeitindesign.com

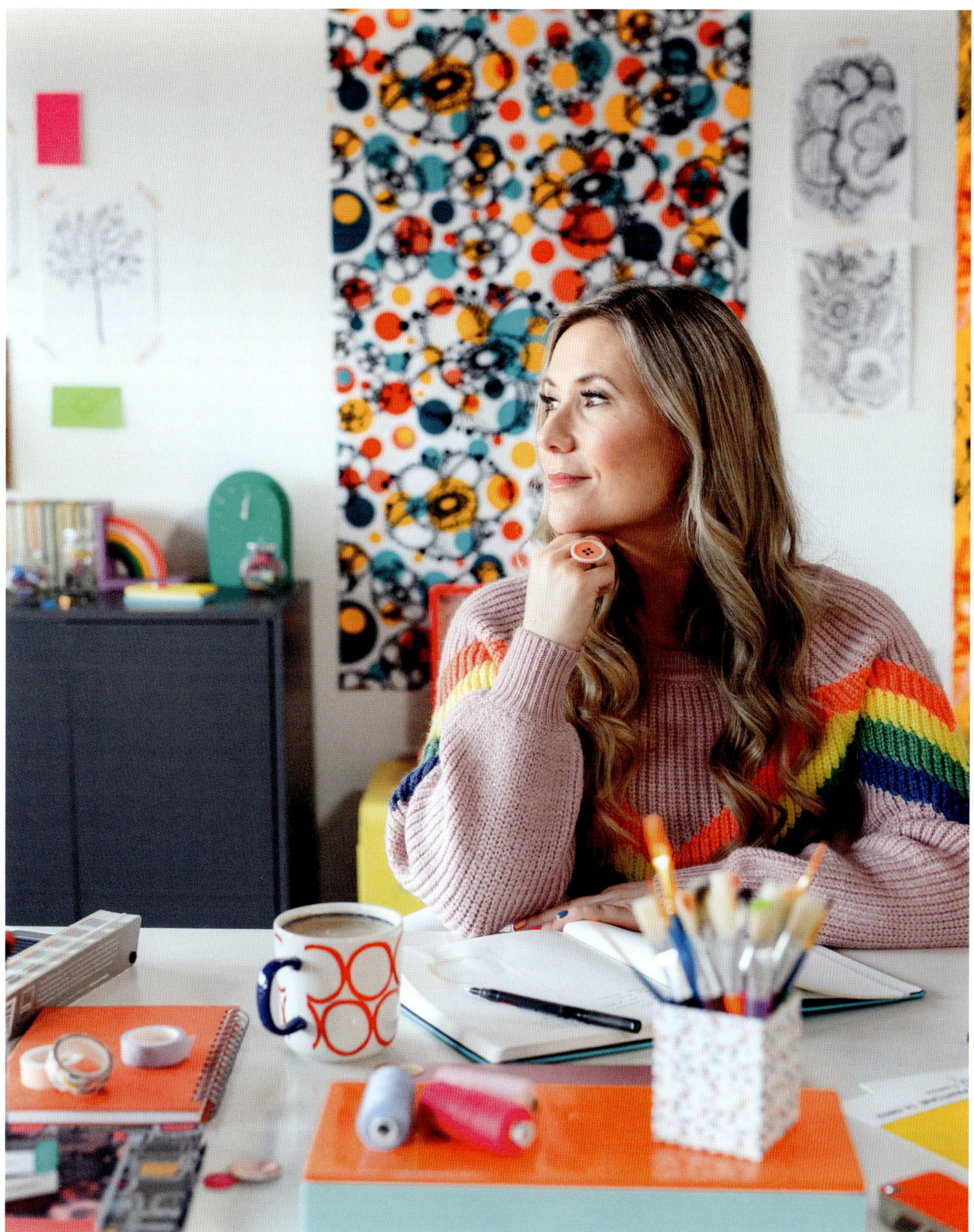

INDEX

D

E

M

N

O

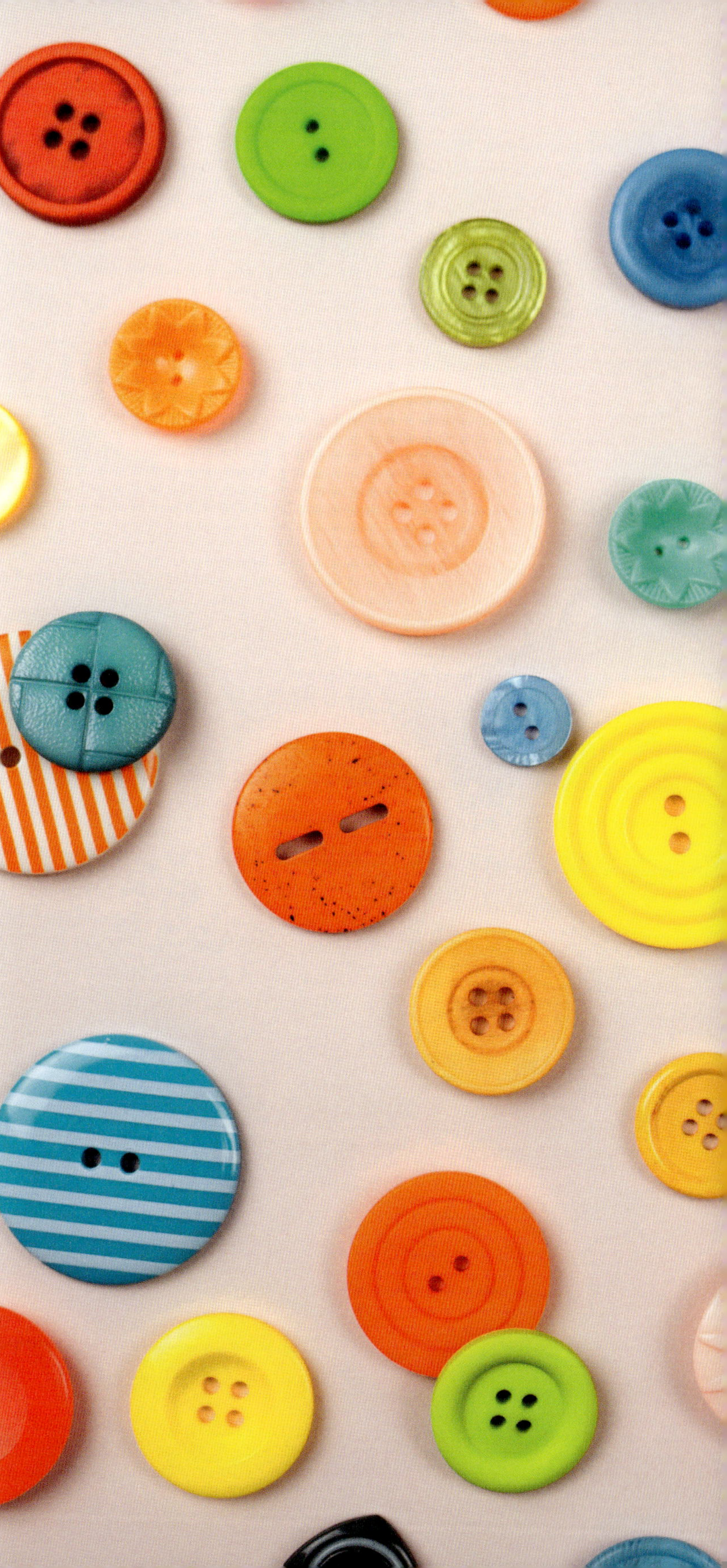

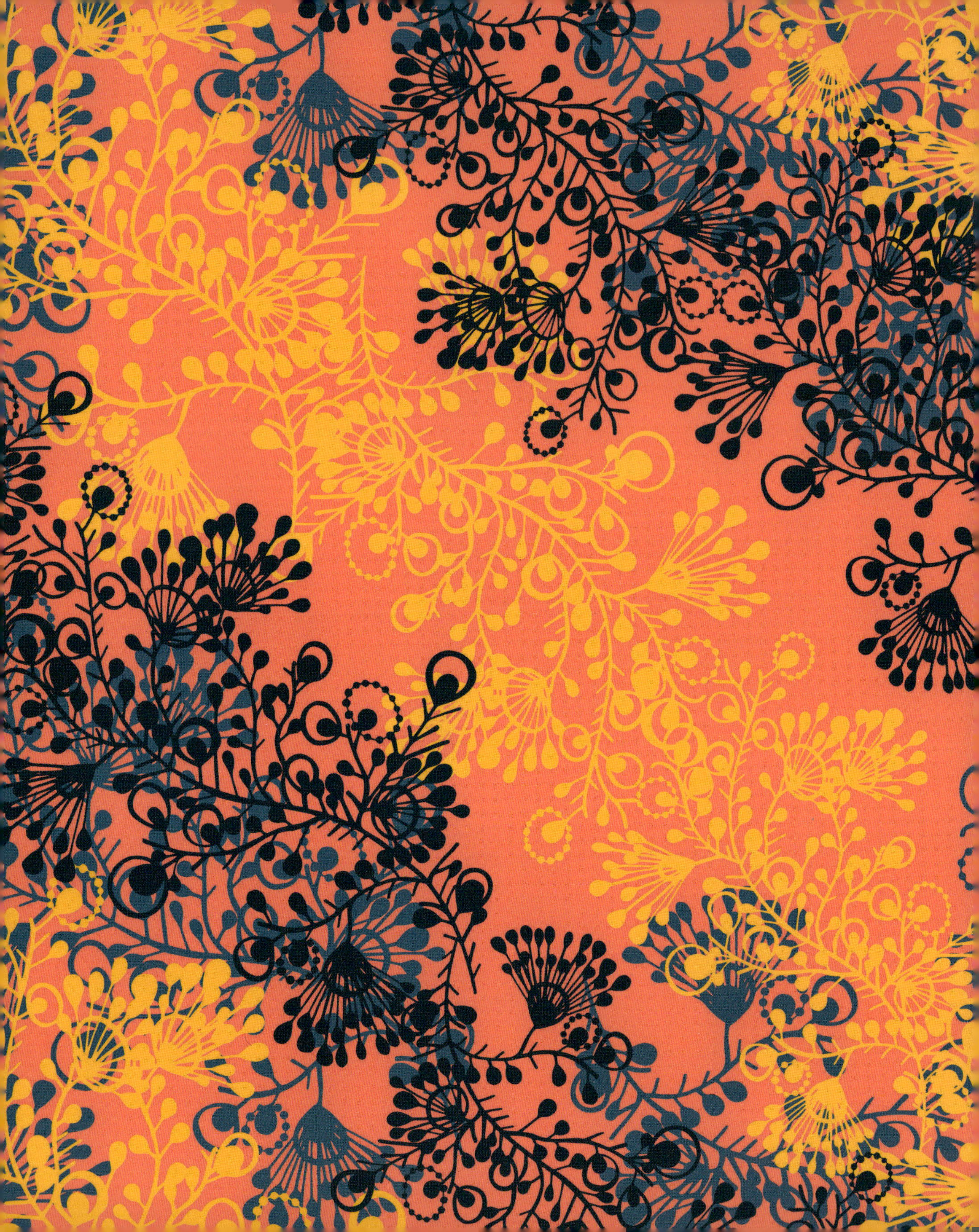